All the Best!

THE BEST
OF THE NEST

Robin's Nest Columns from the Reporter Newspapers

ROBIN CONTE

Happy Reading,

Robin

Published by Springs Publishing, LLC
6065 Roswell Road NE, Suite 225 / Atlanta, GA 30328
www.reporternewspapers.net

Library of Congress Control Number: 2018902966

ISBN 978-0-692-08625-4

Cover Design, Book Layout and Illustrations by Soojin Yang
Author Photo by James Barker

For my father, who laughed with me,
and my mother, who read to me

CONTENTS

— SUMMER —

— FALL

— WINTER

THE BEST OF THE NEST

INTRODUCTION

In these pages, you will find no political commentary.
You will find no advice on parenting or gardening,
no guide to self-actualization, and no cheap shots. You
will find no instructions on food or fashion.

You will find no raging social commentary, although
you might find quiet little rivulets of it here and there.

You won't find any words that you have instructed
your child not to say. For that matter, you will find
nothing you couldn't read with your child, your parent,
or your priest.

What you will find is a collection of columns, neatly
organized into four sections that correspond to the four
seasons of the year: twelve columns per season. And
then, for no extra charge, there's a bonus column. You
may treat these columns as you would small bites on
a tray, for this is a buffet, not a banquet, and you may
sample as you wish, according to your mood.

Behind these pages, you might find a woman with her
tongue planted firmly in her cheek. She is typing away,
remarking on the life we live today and promising to
behave civilly when she is committing her words to print.

And if you read these pages closely enough, you
might find that you share in a story, or two, yourself.

WINTER

1 FENG SHUI CHRISTMAS

t's December, and once again I am decking my halls with Christmas Clutter while asking myself the perennial question: *Why do I do it?* Why do I spend so much energy each year with nutcrackers and knick-knacks? What is it about this month that inspires me to make my house and hands smell like a fir tree?

Well, it's tradition, of course. And it's expectation. If it's a week past Thanksgiving and I haven't pulled out the Advent wreath and the Christmas village, my kids will notice. And they'll ask for it. But most of all, it's me. Just as I wouldn't mail a letter without signing it, I wouldn't feel right if I didn't spread a little of my own signature fa-la-la around our home each December.

Yet, as I surround myself with the sights and scents of the Season—and bargain hunt for Christmas pajamas—I am tempted to simplify. What I really want is a feng shui Christmas. (I'll admit here that I don't know a lot about feng shui except that it's pronounced "fung schwey" and that my father once said that "feng shui is bull shui," but it has something to do with order, balance, and simplification, and that's my only point.)

Simplify, after all, is the buzzword of this generation—along with *yolo* and *podcast*. Simplifying the month of December, however, is a bit of a challenge. But I want to do it. I want to *feng shui* a little "less is more" into the season; I want to nurse my chi with a cup of tea and give my minivan a break. So I'm culling the buying and the baking. I'm decking only *some* of the halls, and I'm letting the crate of snow globes and the four boxes of ornaments go unpacked. I'm weighing wants vs. needs and giving accordingly. I'm simplifying the wish list, and I'm starting with myself.

And that brings me to socks. Personally, all I want for Christmas is a pair of really good socks. So in that way (and in that way only) I am similar to the wise and feng shui-ish Dumbledore. In *Harry Potter and the Sorcerer's*

Stone, he famously looks into the "Mirror of Erised" (that's code for "Mirror of Desire" for the two of you out there who didn't already know that) and claims that the most coveted object of his desire is a pair of thick woolen socks. I can understand that, because a great pair of socks is so hard to find. The irony here is that my husband's first Christmas present to me when we were dating was, in fact, a pair of thick woolen socks. At the time I was not impressed; a pair of socks was not the gift I was hoping for—especially from him. But I married the man anyway, and I still wear the socks. And now, as I've noted, I'd really like a second pair.

It's not a lot to ask for. And I'll admit that I have—in the spirit of order and balance, and sanity—added a few more items to my simple wish list for the season.

From my energy-efficient light bulbs: that extra three years of power that you promised.

From my washing machine: whiter whites and brighter brights. Really.

From my dryer: all of our missing socks.

From my hair: frumpy to fabulous while I sleep.

From yard crews everywhere: silent leaf-blowers.

From my laptop: complete obedience.

From my husband, Mr. Studfinder: the pictures. Hung on the wall. Finally.

From my teenage twin boys: a clean bathroom.

From my son and daughter, who are studying in lands as foreign as Chile and New York: a safe trip home.

Just those things…and world peace.

2 WHAT THE DICKENS?

*D*ickens was on to something. In his classic tale "A Christmas Carol," he writes about the Ghosts of Christmas Past, Present, and Future visiting Ebenezer Scrooge, all in one night. Well, it seems to me that his story isn't all that fanciful because those same three spirits haunt our house annually from December straight through till spring.

The Ghost of Christmas Past lives in the ornament box. I pull out spray-painted pieces of cardboard that are covered with gold pasta and clumps of glitter, and the Spirit whisks me back in time to the years when my children proudly presented them to me. The Spirit enchants photo ornaments of pudgy little baby faces, causing me to recognize those faces hiding behind my sons' facial hair when I squint just so. She transports me as I rifle through the trimmings. Suddenly I am with friends who moved across the country years ago. I am reliving birthdays and anniversaries and hearing choirs I once sung with. I'm seeing children who are thoroughly entertained simply by decoupaging squares of tissue paper onto empty jars of baby food.

The Ghost of Christmas Present is persistent. He enters jovially on Christmas Eve, explodes on Christmas Day with gilded glory, and then on December 26, quietly takes off his boots and settles himself in for the rest of the winter. We find him in the house and yard and in the very air we breathe. He's in the half-packed boxes of decorations and bows that fill the den for weeks, in the scent of Fraser fir candles ever burning, in bowls of red and green M&Ms scattered about, in the needlepoint stocking found mid-February on a knob of the living room door.

Christmas Present lingers by the potted poinsettias as they drop curled leaves onto my kitchen floor and near the gingerbread-man garden flag that flaps in the wind while daffodils push up the earth around it. He will remain until pastel jellybeans and porcelain bunnies appear in April, or he will reluctantly disappear in March during those years when Easter comes early—my tradition being to pack away the final remnants of Christmas on Good Friday.

Christmas Future lives in the pantry and in the freezer. He is sometimes known as the Spirit of Christmas Cookies Yet to Come. He lives in the six bars of Crisco that I have in the cabinet above the refrigerator—purchased anew each December for the past three years—that still may, one day, become biscotti. He is found in the containers of candied fruit that never made their way into batter, but that still hold the promise of the Barefoot Contessa's fruitcake cookies.

Christmas Future also haunts the Christmas mailing list in my Outlook contacts file, which continues to be updated with changed addresses and will be an incredible time-saver next year once we spend three days trying to remember how to get the contacts to print-out on the address labels. And he spooks the closet where 70 percent-off items rest, awaiting the gift-exchanges of Christmases in future years.

For three months, I live in a very crowded house. The Spirits jostle for position in my kitchen, den, and basement, and then, being ethereal creatures, manage to occupy my head and my credit card bills, as well. I find myself, as Mr. Scrooge professed at the end of The Carol, to be living "in the Past, the Present, and the Future." Perhaps it is as the Spirits intended, but there is really nothing I can do about it.

I mean, what the Dickens?

3

THE DIFFERENCE
BETWEEN
MEN AND WOMEN

I'm driving down North Georgia Highway 515 with my husband, and we pass the sprawling store that we always pass, the one that's a combination of barn and warehouse. It's marked with a sign sporting two massive, spurred cowboy boots and the enticing advertisement: "Western Wear, Tack & Feed."

My husband spoke. "See that place? I drove by it last month with my brother, and he told me he went in there."

"Oh, really?" I replied, honestly intrigued by what

might lie beyond its barn-sized doors and ruminating about the meaning of *tack*. "What did he say about it?"

"Nothing. He just said he went in there."

And that right there is the difference between men and women. Two men are in a car together for a two-hour road trip, and that is the extent of their conversation.

Put two women in a car together and throw out that line, and it would serve as a springboard for conversation that would last for the 1½ hour remainder of the journey.

We would talk about (most likely in this order) tack & feed and the meanings thereof, jeans, boots, fashions, changing fashions, country music, pop music, Justin Bieber, our children, our children, our children, schools, teachers, sports, weight gain, boot camp, our children, yoga, diets, Obamacare, mothers, life coaches, books, appliances, and our children. And that's if there were only *two* women in the car. With each additional woman the length of the conversation would grow exponentially, so that if there were *four* women in the car, that one initial comment would take us clear to Idaho.

My husband is constantly astounded by the fact that women are almost never at a loss for something to say, and I am constantly astounded by the fact that men almost always are.

Some call it "the gift of gab," and I do consider it a gift. I can cover more topics during one hour with my dental hygienist than I do during three days with my husband, and this is of course, while my teeth are being cleaned.

That is why book groups are so popular with the ladies. They serve as another reason to get together and talk. We gather over food and beverage and we *do*, in fact, have a discussion about the book (because somebody's bound to have read it), and then we spin off into various conversations, in the way that *CSI* spins off into various new series.

Book groups will never catch on with men. There are men who read, of course; there are men who will find a book they really like, but they're not going to sit around with each other on a Tuesday night and talk about it. If they're going to sit around together, they'll choose an activity (such as watching a ball game) that requires them *not* to talk, but only to jump up occasionally and yell.

Which brings me to Super Bowl parties. They are the perfect crowd pleaser: they provide a non-verbal activity for the men while also providing another opportunity for the women to gather in the kitchen and talk.

I can hear the cries of "sexist!" mounting throughout the city, but I do realize that there are mold-breakers out there. You can find the occasional woman who knows that there are sixty scoreboard minutes in a football game, just as you can find the occasional man who is interested in discussing *The Fault in Our Stars*. But I'm not squabbling over differences—I'm embracing them. We women are social networkers of the most extraordinary sort; communication is a valuable and essential skill, and women excel at it.

So, good for us.

Now I know that the Super Bowl is on in the next room, though I don't know who's playing, and I don't know the score.

But I'd love for you to sit down next to me while we sip some wine together and have a chat.

THIS THING CALLED LOVE

hen my twins were but elementary school boys, one of them developed a crush on a girl. Upon learning this sweet tidbit, I did what I do in embarrassing situations—pry information from the twin brother. So I asked twin brother, "Does *she* like *him*?" To which he responded enthusiastically, "Yes! It's like a *miracle*!"

Even at the tender age of ten, my son recognized the simple wonder of requited love: that returned affection is a phenomenon not to be taken lightly. It doesn't happen every day, it doesn't even happen every lifetime, and if and when it does happen, it is a small miracle.

So what is this thing called love, and how does it stay alive? Four children and a couple of decades after my own wedding day, I feel like I should have some answers. But I don't. I do, however, have some thoughts.

I heard in a high school English class that "love is friendship caught fire," and I have yet to come across a tidier definition. It has taken a whole heap of friendship and just enough sparks to keep this marriage going.

It has also been said that love isn't an emotion, it's a commitment, and a recent viewing of *Fiddler on the Roof* at a neighborhood playhouse brought that statement to my mind.

It was the song "Do You Love Me?" that did it. In the song, our protagonist Tevye asks Golde, his wife of twenty-five years by an arranged marriage, "Do you love me?" There is such poignancy in that question and in the fact that after twenty-five years of marriage, he must ask and she avoids answering.

She responds with a list of domestic chores that she has done dutifully throughout their life together. He continues prodding, and Golde replies, "For twenty-five years I've lived with him, fought him, starved with him. For twenty-five years, my bed is his. If that's not love, what is?" Finally, they both admit that yes, they do love each other after all, and that (this is the part that really chokes me up) "after twenty-five years...it's nice to know."

I cried, as I do every time I hear it. And I realize that commitment is exactly what Golde was singing about. Commitment was the glue that held those two initial strangers together, and from that commitment, love grew.

Something else about the lyrics struck me: that period of time that seems so noteworthy when set to music and sung onstage is the milestone that my husband and I have just hit. I think now of our own ups and downs, the years raising children together, the years of supporting each other in our trials and achievements, of working out our differences...the years spent learning who we married. And I am astounded that a quarter of a century has passed like a wisp.

Last summer, my husband and I celebrated our twenty-fifth anniversary. It's been a bit like a marathon...and a lot like a miracle.

5

ON EARRINGS AND IPHONES

hen my daughter was nearing the end of her high school career and had a Senior Day Off, we did a mother-daughter thing. We got our ears pierced. She had held out for eighteen years, and I had held out for, um, longer than that. We went to Claire's and perched on high-top chairs facing each other, hugged teddy bears and waited for the big staple gun to power through our lobes. It's how memories are made.

I never really wanted to get my ears pierced. I didn't see a need to have any more holes in my body. And I probably wouldn't have done it otherwise, but piercing in tandem with your daughter is one of those rare opportunities that you don't pass up—like when your son asks you to go shopping with him, or your husband wants to schedule a sitting for a family photo.

Aside from the unwanted extra orifices, my biggest aversion to the whole piercing process was the fact that I knew that once I did it, there would be earrings. I would start buying earrings, and people would give me earrings for birthdays and Christmas and Mother's Day, and I would begin to like that. I would learn to linger at the jewelry counter over a selection of dangling objects that never interested me before. It would just be another way to spend thirty bucks a pop. It would be unavoidable.

That's essentially the same reason that I didn't want an iPhone. I knew that once I entered the world of smartThings, I would be opening a floodgate to a constant river of distractions and apps for distractions. And there would be no turning back.

I had a phone I was happy with, much to the chagrin of anyone who tried to communicate with me on it. It was like a 1992 Subaru. It was reliable, yet old and outdated and not much coveted. It had a warped keypad that I used occasionally to text "k" and "here," and nothing more. But it I could drop it roughly forty-two times a day (and I did), then literally pick up the pieces, slam them back into place, and redial.

It was a ten-year-old Nokia, and it didn't do much of anything but make calls. It didn't give me directions, get my emails, take pictures, or answer any burning questions I had about Bastille Day. It didn't even "flip" or "slide." It just sat there, easily, in my back pocket with its indestructible self, giving me a serendipitous jolt whenever someone buzzed me with a phone call.

But as it creaked on in its years and lost parts through my constant dropping of it, it also slowly lost its ability to function, even as a phone. And I eventually had to admit that no one could hear on it very well, not even me.

So a few years ago, when my husband presented me with a snazzy new iPhone4S (because I wasn't worthy of a 5) complete with the promise of a new service provider, I laid my trusty Nokia to rest in my bedside table and entered the world of Distracted Adults.

Sure enough, now I'm playing with Pandora when I should be working. I'm checking emails while I'm supposedly exercising. And I've joined my peers in relentless texting. We're all like a bunch of delinquents who are passing notes in class.

Texts come in while I'm brushing my teeth or paying bills or making dinner, and like a passel of whining children who are yanking at my legs, they beg for attention. I'll glance at my screen and find a pressing question or an irresistible Bitmoji staring back at me, so I stop what I'm doing to text back—taking the time to correct the self-correct and choose just the right emoji—and a flurry of exchanges ensues that completely spins me off task. For all of our efforts to live in the moment, the smart-Phone is the ultimate antithesis.

I've devised a system, though, a type of positive reinforcement designed to limit myself from the tantalizing distractions that this device provides: if I can go through an entire day without messing with my phone while working or cooking or eating or exercising...I'll buy myself a new pair of earrings.

6 DOES THIS PHONE MAKE MY FINGERS LOOK FAT?

I think I'm in pretty good shape. I walk daily, I work out regularly, I do sit-ups and push-ups and squats and lunges; I've advanced to the Half-Lord of the Fishes pose in my yoga class.

But I've become self-conscious about a part of my body that never bothered me before. And I'm beginning to wonder: *Does this phone make my fingers look fat?*

I'm getting a bit sensitive about it because I've been making fat-finger calls since I got it. It's not that hard to do. I'll go to call one person on my favorites list and because she's sandwiched between two other people on a smooth and glossy screen, I'll hit the wrong favorite. It's getting to be a problem, especially when I fat-finger call someone who is out of the country.

My old phone never did that. It fit me just fine. It was like a well-worn, relaxed-fit pair of jeans; it was comfy and roomy and it made me feel good about myself and about the size of my text fingers. It had plenty of wiggle room. It was a ten-year-old Nokia with a smashed-in keyboard, but that had its advantages. For one thing, I could text with my thumbnail. That old-timey keyboard allowed for precision hits.

I got a skinny new phone a few years ago, but it's just too tight. Worse, it has a virtual keyboard that needs a fleshy finger to place a call. This updated yet unforgiving keyboard wants fleshy but not *too* fleshy—it wants a perfectly shaped, size-four text finger.

At least it has gotten accustomed to my digital heft, and it knows that when I type *Vsn hou fi?* I mean *Can you go?* I'm learning, too. I've started texting in the wrong word so it will self-correct to the right word because that's faster than trying to hit all right letters.

I never used to have a problem with my fingers overlapping onto another contact or another letter, but now they're spreading all over the keyboard. I feel like my fingers have developed muffin top. It's really unnerving.

I know, I know. I need to upsize to the "boyfriend-fit"

version of a smartphone, the one that's designed for full-figured fingers. But I can't bear to part with this tiny little number that fits so perfectly into the back pocket of my jeans and the side pouch of my purse.

So I'm going to take matters into my own hands—literally. I'm going to lose that finger flab! I've decided to put my digits through a good workout every day. I want the fingers of a twenty-year-old.

I found a set of easy finger exercises guaranteed to slim those digits down to stylus shape.

I'll warm them up with a series of stretches and then move to the toning and tightening. I'll run them through a strenuous game of finger soccer for the aerobic component of the program, and then it'll be time for the cool down.

And while I FLEX *two three four*, STRETCH *two three four*, LIFT *two three four*, BEND *two three four*, please tell me that it's not me... it's my phone.

7 A BIT OF BITMOJI

To the absolute horror of my children, I now have a Bitmoji.

And I finally figured out that a very effective way to get back at the offspring for the all years of toddler tantrums, teen angst, and post-graduate anxiety (and let's not forget the combined seventy-three hours of labor) is to bombard them with Bitmojis…constant streams of cringe-worthy Bitmojis.

It's like seeing me in a bathing suit. They hate it.

A Bitmoji, as you know, is basically an emoji cubed. It's a smiley-face unleashed in its animated form. It's an iPaper-doll with attitude. It's an app on your smartPhone that creates a cartoon avatar of yourself and comes to life as your alter-ego, compete with your face, your hair, your eyes, and your wardrobe of choice. It was apparently invented for twelve-year-old girls and middle-aged women, but now practically everyone has one.

One of the allures of Bitmojidom is that you can create your own and ostensibly personalize it to look just like you. But who are we kidding? It will look much better than you do. Faster than you can say "Botox," you can choose a wrinkle-free complexion; in the time it takes to google "Mediterranean diet," you can give your cyber-self a flab-free body. And then you can revert to your inner child and dress your little bitty Bitmjoi.

I've done all that, and I have produced a Bitmoji that is way hotter than I am. She dresses better than I do, too. I'm actually getting jealous of my Bitmoji because she looks good in everything, even outfits I haven't worn since I was twenty-one, like a midriff top and cutoff shorts. She's fab in the Wonder Woman getup, and she totally rocks the Turtleneck & Chain. She even looks good in a broken eggshell.

My Bitmoji is also more coordinated than I am, more adventurous than I am, more competent than I am, and wittier than I am. Plus, she has a lot more fun than I do. I don't know if I can live up to her.

But I'm still going to keep her around, since she comes in very handy. This is because everything is cute in Bitmoji speak. You see, a Bitmoji is like an Irish accent, in that you can say anything with one and get away with it. You want to break up? Say you're running late? Dis someone? Ask someone to the prom? There's a Bitmoji for that. And there's a Bitmoji that says, "There's a Bitmoji for that."

Which brings me back to annoying the kids. Why just ask them to call me when I can send my Bitmoji with a megaphone to do the dirty work? Or I could opt for a sassy message in the form of my Bitself flopping on the couch, asking the colorful question "What Up Fam?" If they're not sending me photos or following through on various tasks, I can admonish them with my Bitself dressed as a carrot top and threaten to send more.

Once they see me in Bitform, striking a John Travolta-Saturday Night Fever pose beneath a disco ball, they'll beg for mercy.

Revenge is sweet.

8 LIVING IN THE ZONE

here's been a lot of talk about The Zone these days.

There's a Zone exercise plan. There's a Zone life-plan. There's a Zone diet. There is so much zoning going on that it's a bit tricky to determine exactly what "The Zone" is.

As far as I can tell, The Zone is either a brand name or a state of mind—or both.

It's a way of life and a way of eating. It's a college student's Nirvana—being able to read a text book passage and "get it" the first time. It's that rare and coveted condition of operating at full mental or physical capacity. It's being in a place that's free of stress or distraction or Hall and Oates playing in the background.

What I really want to know is, where is this Zone and why can't I live there?

For most of my adult life, I have lived in lesser zones. When my kids were toddlers, I lived in the No-Zone. And for the past few decades, I've lived in the Uh-Oh Zone.

That's the zone where one child will always come down with a stomach ache and a 102-degree fever on the day before the family vacation.

Where, if we are running late for school, the car battery will die or a bird will fly into the house.

Where thunder rumbles exactly thirty minutes after the start of a neighborhood swim meet and continues at a steady pattern of every twenty-one minutes thereafter for the next two hours.

Where, after I have arrived home from running errands at seven different stores, there will still be a child who tells me that he needs notebook paper and cupcakes for school the next morning.

I'm ready for a new zone.

I want to live in a Zone Of My Own. I want to live in a place where I can get toned while texting, where the route I choose to Costco always has the best flow of traffic, where decisions are made without angst.

I want to live in The Zone where I please all of the people all of the time.

In this place, my hair always looks good and my indoor plants live a long and full life. Dust doesn't settle quite so quickly, and the stones on my front porch gather no moss. My flowerbeds are surrounded by an invisible shield that protects them from squirrels, chipmunks, rabbits, deer, coyotes, and basketballs.

And my internet never shuts down.

In this Zone, we can always find the remote.

I want to live in The Zone where I can make a complete dinner without setting off the smoke alarm.

Where cream cheese and yogurt last for three months past their expiration date, and "customer service" thrives wherever I shop.

Where every purchase I make has been fairly traded and is ecologically sound—and costs less than ten dollars.

Where I am always the first one in the carpool line, no matter when I leave the house.

Where scintillating conversation and witty repartee flow freely from my mouth and I can instantly summon the perfect sparkling comeback.

And my internet never shuts down.

I don't want to live in the zone that's narrated by Rod Serling—I feel like I've wandered into that zone often enough. I want to dwell in the place where my coupons are always good and fifteen-minute power naps really work.

And I am always appreciated.

If you know where this place is, please tell me. Because my internet just shut down, and I am zoning out.

9 DEATH OF A LAPTOP

My computer died today.

I came downstairs to give it my morning greeting, powering it awake while brewing my coffee and waiting for us to go through our simultaneous morning routine of yawning and stretching and coaxing our groggy eyes open until we face each other, so I can scroll through emails and daily news, mug in hand.

But I went downstairs this morning, powered it awake, and nothing happened. The screen remained a blank hazy blue, with no morning greetings, no field-of-lavender screensaver, no desktop. I rebooted it, and this time the screen was not even an eerie blue, it was solid black—it was collapse-of-a-supernova black. It had contracted the dreaded Black Screen, which is the bubonic plague of all things digital.

So my husband and I hustled over to the computer store because I hoped that they could fix it. My husband, however, announced that it was time for me to buy a new laptop. I really felt like that wouldn't be necessary, reasoning that I've only had the thing about three and a half years, which in my mind is just long enough to get it comfortably broken-in, but then it dawned on me that computer years are akin to dog years, only about four times longer, meaning that a computer ages roughly twenty-eight times faster than the average human.

I was indeed lured into buying a new laptop rather than trying to repair the old one because 1) my laptop is ninety-eight in human years, 2) they said they could transfer all the data by tomorrow night, and 3) I am gullible.

I could have been happy about getting a brand-spanking new computer, but I like my old one; it's comfortable and familiar, like a favorite pair of jeans. And actually, I think that buying a new PC falls somewhere between buying a new pair of jeans and buying a new house—and the cost of it falls somewhere between the two, as well.

You know that the new jeans will never fit like the old ones; you know there will be that breaking-in period and that something about the rise or the length or the back pockets will be "updated." And you might be excited about a brand-new home, but there's the hassle with the move, and you know that all of your furniture won't fit and you'll have to replace some of it, and that there's always the risk of something getting lost in the move.

And there are some things about that old house that you're just going to miss, like your wallpaper. I like my fields-of-lavender wallpaper. And I'm wondering if it's been discontinued and will I ever be able to see it again?

So currently, while awaiting the data transfer to my new computer, I'm typing on an old ASUS Notebook that I unearthed and that's about eighty-four in human years. It is exactly as functional as an actual spiral-bound notebook, but not as responsive and with less storage capacity.

Now if you are like me, you manage your home, your business, your finances, your social life, your children's lives, and your distractions from your personal computer. When I sit down to mine each morning, I feel like I'm in the captain's seat of the Starship *Enterprise*, and it's fitted with a cup holder. Equipped now with only my feeble Notebook and my outdated smartPhone, I feel like I'm running my world from the bottom of a La Brea tar pit, armed with a walkie-talkie and a slide rule.

There's nothing left to do but put on my favorite pair of jeans and wait for moving day.

10 GRAMMAR SNOB

I am a coffee snob. I am a chocolate snob. And when it comes to grammar and punctuation, I am an annoying snob.

I am one of those people who can ruin a good outing by complaining about improperly punctuated signage. Put more genteelly, I have a cultivated appreciation for a properly punctuated sentence and for pronouns in their objective form.

So in my column for today, I am going to extol the virtues of grammar and punctuation. I am going to use words and phrases such as "aforementioned," "as it were," and "grammatically speaking." I am going to use the serial comma. And, as a bonus, I am going to give you a free grammar lesson.

Here it is: "To you and I" is grammatically incorrect because "to" is a preposition and thus takes the objective form of a pronoun. "To you and me" is correct, grammatically speaking. Always.

There. Now that that's out of the way, I will proceed to signage.

I enjoy a pithy phrase as much as the next person, whether it's embroidered on a kitchen towel, stamped on a stack of cocktail napkins, or painted on reclaimed wood. For instance, I bought a sign for a sommelier friend of mine that read "A meal without wine is breakfast." It's funny and correctly written, so it passes my test.

But not all signs are so spot-on. I will find signs with misplaced modifiers and participles dangling all over the place, signs that pay no attention to punctuation (witness: "Weekends are a girls best friend"). I find others, such as "Blessed," "Family," and "Chardonnay," that apparently have no idea what to do with a phrase and play it safe with single words.

Then I will come across a plaque that's selling for $24.95, and, while I might agree with the sentiment, I will develop a nervous tic at the sight of a poorly punctuated phrase and will continue exhibiting physical symptoms of stress at the mere memory of it until I am at last compelled to correct it in writing…and perhaps publish that correction, as it were. Take this sign, for instance: "But first coffee."

Now I ask you, what is first coffee? Is first coffee a drink that is served on a first date while performing first aid for a first class first impression?

No. No, it is not.

What I want is a sign that says this: But first, coffee. Add a comma and you have created a sign that I can get behind. If you really want me to buy it, you can write this: But first…coffee. That gives me more of a pause, more of an "ah and sip" moment with which to begin my day.

And because my theme today is splitting hairs, I will continue with an example of a questionably punctuated humorous sign: "You had me at merlot." This, of course, is a clever and amusing play on the line in *Jerry Maguire*, "You had me at 'hello,'" and thus, in my grammatically uptight world, should be punctuated with "merlot" in quotation marks. Therefore, I believe that the sign should be written like this: You had me at "merlot," which would naturally cause sales of the aforementioned sign to plummet.

And annihilating sales of signage is not my goal here, for I respect anyone's right to print words on wood and make a few bucks. I only want to heighten your awareness of signage punctuation to the point that when you pass a poorly punctuated one, you, too, will develop a nervous tic.

Beyond that, my goal is simply to hold your interest in grammar and punctuation enough to keep you watching for my next column, which will be dedicated to the Oxford comma.

11 OXFORD COMMA

I confessed in my last column, "Grammar Snob," that I am, in fact, a Grammar Snob. I am one of those people (there are three of us) who finds robust humor in Jack Sparrow's use of parallel structure in *Pirates of the Caribbean: The Curse of the Black Pearl*, where he states, "I think we've all arrived at a very special place. Spiritually, ecumenically, grammatically." Ha! Ha! I'm giggling right now.

But I reserve special affection for the comma. It is so often misused, unused, and underused, I feel that the least I can do is devote 675 words to the little guy. Honestly, the comma is an invention of our civilized world that is not unlike the zipper: even though we might occasionally get hung-up on it, it truly makes our lives easier.

Ironically, another construct of our modern world is hastening the demise of our friend, comma. I am referring, of course, to texting. You can find a teenager at a Barry Manilow concert more often than you'll find a comma in a text. My texts, however, will come to you properly punctuated. I can't help it.

I take heart in the fact that I'm in good company regarding my respect for the comma, as there is an Oscar Wilde anecdote that has been entertaining Grammar Snobs for decades. The story goes that when Wilde was questioned smugly about what kind of work he did all day, he responded that he spent most of the day putting in a comma and the rest of the day taking it out.

Go, Oscar! I do, too! (Or is it, "Go Oscar; I do too"?)

Anyhoo, then my editor gets in the game with me, because I'll put a comma in, and he'll take it out.

I happen to enjoy writing the occasional long, breezy and rhythmic, free-flowing sentence—not so free-flowing and stream–of-consciousness as James Joyce, per se, but lengthy enough to cover the lumpy parts and loose enough to be comfortable, like a swing-top.

But my editor doesn't like long sentences. He likes them short. He likes them punchy. He likes them short and punchy. He takes out commas and puts in periods.

This brings me to another comma entirely, which is the serial comma, a.k.a. the Oxford comma, my absolute favorite comma of all. I think of it as a rare gem when I see it glowing brightly in its perfect setting between the penultimate word in a series and a conjunction. My editor, however, uses the Associated Press comma, which is invisible. So I'll write a phrase such as "planes, trains, and automobiles," and as soon as I pass it along to my editor, my attentively placed serial comma (the one after "trains") will disappear like my kids when it's time to do yardwork.

I maintain that the conjunction is not enough. Imagine us walking through a garden, stopping along the way to smell the roses, as it were, and then when we near the end of our stroll, we are shoved right past the final bed of flowers. Well, that would be rude. It's the same way with the written word. We walk along through a series, pausing politely after each word or phrase in it, and then we hit the no-man's land of comma blankage and stumble clumsily, head-first into the final word. It's madness.

My affection for the serial comma was rekindled several months ago when I learned about a court case in Maine that involved said comma; it had to do with dairy workers and the tasks they performed that would or would not garner them overtime pay. Without going into journalistic details, I will tell you that the final two items on the list of tasks ineligible for overtime pay were not separated by a comma. The judge stated, "For want of a comma, we have this case," and, in fact, for want of a comma, the dairy workers won.

The devil is in the details, and the clarity is in the comma.

12 AGING POLITELY

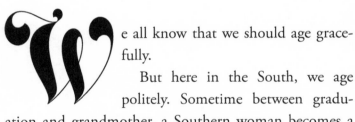e all know that we should age gracefully.

But here in the South, we age politely. Sometime between graduation and grandmother, a Southern woman becomes a "ma'am." That's when we know that we have become a "woman of a certain age."

I don't remember what age I was when I morphed from "girl" to "ma'am," but somewhere in the thick of ma'amhood, I became a "young lady" again. And I must say that being referred to as a "young lady" when you're in your fifties is about as jarring as being called "ma'am" when you're in your twenties.

I was in a grocery store when I became a "young lady" once more; I was stocking-up for my household full of kids, and I'm sure that the employee who used the term was trying extra-hard to be un-offensive, but I didn't like the term at all. Really, that's not a term anybody likes. Young ladies don't even like to be called young ladies. Maybe three-year olds do, but I think the address loses its appeal once they pass the age of five.

What really bothered me about the term is that it felt like the fellow who used it was going a bit too far in the opposite direction. Because the thing is, I know I'm not a young lady. I know I'm not tripping through the streets of Paris with Gigi and Madeline. I find it just a wee bit patronizing.

I pondered this a while longer, as I loaded and un-loaded my groceries, and wondered, when a middle-aged gentleman steps up to the register, does that employee call him a "young man"? I think not. What about "young laddie"? No, that would not fly, not even in Scotland.

Maybe men don't get as bristled at "sir," anyway. "Sir" has a certain grandeur, a royal connotation that carries it beyond the scope of age-inference. Maybe "ma'am" is a problem because it's an abbreviation; maybe if people went around using the full-throttled "madam," the term would connote something loftier than mere middle age. Even though "ma'am," according to Sir Mister Webster, is "used to speak to the queen or woman of high rank," in this country, at least, it is not a term that evokes refined appreciation. Rather, it generates a huffy "How do you know I'm a ma'am?" type of response.

It's kind of a shame, and that brings me round to my topic, in that aging politely is becoming harder to do. Somewhere, somehow, good manners have become distasteful.

People shy away from being respectful because they're afraid of being offensive. We teach our kids manners, but their manners can be taken as insults. And the root of the problem is that none of us wants to be perceived as "old," so we pretend like we've discovered the fountain of youth by tossing out a moniker.

The fact is, we don't know how to address each other anymore.

What do you call your parents' friends, once you've grown up and moved out of the house and have children of your own? How do you address the couple you used to babysit for, once you're employing a babysitter yourself?

There are some monikers that will never change. My former Girl Scout leader, for instance, will always and forever be "Mrs. C" to all of us fully grown Girl Scouts. My parents' friends will remain "Mr." or "Mrs." unless and until they implore me to address them otherwise. Teachers, no matter what their ages, will be addressed using their surnames, by *moi*.

And when someone, especially a young lady or a young man, addresses me as "ma'am," I will need to smile graciously and give thanks to the vigilant parents who raised their children with good manners—manners enough to help me age politely.

SPRING

13 GROSS

"Hurry boys! Come see this gross thing!"
They came running, of course, and I couldn't believe the words that had just come out of my mouth. But this was a bonding opportunity that I couldn't pass up.

The fragrant plug-in that had been lodged into the laundry room outlet in order to de-stinkify the place was breeding moths. I had finally unplugged it in order to replace the flashing Christmas tree light with a yellow daisy decoration, and when I did, a swarm of tiny insects flew from the outlet and the back of the device.

I knew it had been plugged in for a while, but I didn't for a second think that it had been there long enough to produce life.

It's telling, that my first thought was to call my boys. I've spent twenty-four years bonding with my children over disgusting things.

When we adults are in our early stages of parenting—the gullible years—we think that we'll bond with our young bundles of joy over all of the glorious wonders that the world has to offer: the sunsets, the seascapes, the purple mountain majesties, and all that.

But I've learned that if I want to get a reaction from my kids, a thing has to be gross. And if it's not gross, it must be dangerous, or, at the very least, downright weird.

They'll have a contest over who can peel off the longest piece of sunburnt skin.

They'll battle each other with overgrown toenails.

They won't pull out their smartThings to text a photo of a lovely butterfly, but if I find a snake on the deck, they'll come running with iPhones at the ready.

On one family vacation, all four of my kids were yawning through a glass-blowing demonstration, but when I announced that the bathrooms were fitted with brushes that popped out of the wall to clean the toilet seats, they all perked-up and scurried to the stalls.

I think we humans have to age into appreciation. I

think that happens around the time that afternoon naps become appealing. Until then, we are entertained by the bizarre.

My oldest son once gave me a Mother's Day gift of handmade organic soaps and bath salts. Their therapeutic scents were specially chosen for me (based on my taste in music, incidentally), and they all promised healing and energizing properties.

One of them was designed to massage; it was filled with essential-muscle-relaxing-oils and crusted with nubby beans to work out the kinks. It was my favorite of the soaps, but after a few weeks of trying to work it into a lather, some of the fairly-traded beans started washing off. Around the same time, I noticed that the shower water was backing up. Then one morning I went to collect the bath towels, and to my horror, I discovered that the beans had sprouted in the shower drain.

What did I do? I immediately called my son, of course, who was fully impressed. And he doesn't impress easily. We couldn't believe what his soap had done.

It turned out that it was not a soap at all—it was simply a "massage bar," and I was never supposed to *just add water*. We could have grown a salad if we had only known.

I unscrewed the drain so that we could lean in and get the full view of grass growing from below the tiles. It was a magical moment. We hovered there above the grout, mother and son sharing in the spectacle, and we gazed and guffawed in disgust.

Is this column getting too gross for you?

Call your kids and bond over it.

14 SPRING CLEANING MAGIC

*T*here's good news for all of you spring cleaners out there. Cleaning has been elevated to "life-changing magic."

This status is due to a little manual by Marie Kondo that I'm sure you've heard of, as it has spawned another book, a journal, a Japanese TV show, numerous talk-show demonstrations, and a small cult. It climbed its way to the top of the *New York Times* Best Sellers list a few years ago with the seductive title *The Life-Changing Magic of Tidying Up: The Japanese Art of Decluttering and Organizing*.

Life-changing is a tall order. When I think "life-changing," a few things spring to mind—my new dishwasher and whole ground flaxseed meal, for instance (and then when I stop to reflect, I hastily add "husband and kids," as if someone is actually checking my mental list of life-changers, but in fact, spouse and children are so life-changing they should have their own special category).

At any rate, I had heard of the book due to its stint on The List, but I didn't actually buy it because I don't have room for another thing in my cluttered home. Instead, I got the CliffsNotes version from a friend (thank you, Cathy) who explained to me that the gist of the process—the litmus test, if you will, for discarding or keeping an item—is not if you might wear it again one day, or if it was given to you by your college roommate, or if your son made the thing in summer camp when he was nine years old, or if you think you might be able to grow basil in it….no. The fundamental question you must ask yourself about a particular item is this: *Does it give you joy?*

That's not only a tantalizing question, but a liberating approach to cleaning out a closet. And to add a bit of Japanese-art authenticity, along with some primeval excitement, to the entire expunging process, you are to hold said item to your heart and wait until you feel the joy actually "spark."

Bear in mind, please, that I have not read the book and am not offering a review or even instructions; I am merely intrigued by the method and was interested in testing the joy-sparking potential of my own wardrobe. I decided that I'd clean first and then read the book to see if I did it right.

Besides, if tidying up could change my life half as much as a new appliance, I was willing to give it a go.

I went directly to my own closet, and it was initially a bit tricky, but then I applied the joy-inducing standard with increasingly giddy abandon and, I must say, it was indeed liberating.

At first I tried holding a particular item to my chest, and sometimes a pair of jeans did spark a flicker of joy (but only because they reminded me of how they used to fit ten years ago), and then the joyful spark flickered into something like defeat, and then I flung the jeans into the discard pile, which sparked the flicker of joy once again. And so it went, through the row of clothes hanging in my closet, until I felt myself becoming lighthearted and ready—nay, *eager*—to move on to shoes.

By now I was so adept at the technique that I didn't even need to take the time to hold any shoes to my heart. All that was needed was to eyeball a pair of twenty-year-old Nine West black patent leather pumps with four-inch heels, and my feet veritably swelled in pain at the memory of the way they felt after standing in them for fifteen minutes at a cocktail party. Out they went—and another six pairs of old, deteriorating shoes along with them. By this time, I was practically levitating with joy.

Because, as I surveyed my freshly purged closet, I thought to myself, "It's time to go shopping!"

15 THE DRAWER

The other day, in honor of spring, I decided to clean something. Not wanting to overwhelm myself, I resolved to start small and set an attainable goal. After all, I did want to set myself up for success.

So I cleaned out a drawer.

But it wasn't an ordinary drawer, it was THE drawer. You know the one—it's the black hole of the kitchen, the catch-all place for Things That You'll Get To Later. It's The Drawer of Misfit Junk.

Cleaning it out is like hiking down the Grand Canyon. You pass layers of time as you go, and you stop along the way to excavate and reminisce when you hit the lower levels.

You start at the most negotiable outcroppings—the piles of take-out menus and Band-Aids. You continue, trekking by a new address card for an old friend, a boutonniere from somebody's wedding, and a mini-fan that hangs around your neck, sprays water, and was purchased for a summer concert at Chastain Park. And then you reach that birthday card that you bought for your neighbor and put where you were sure you'd find it, but when her birthday rolled around, you couldn't, and so were finally compelled to run out and get another one (which was not nearly as perfect as this one that you just found).

Next you hit the Layer of Random Photos. You find a picture from a homecoming tailgate, photos that your mother sent you of the flowers you sent her, proofs from your oldest child's high school yearbook shoot, and a few photos of people you are sure you never knew.

You stop for rest and nourishment, because you have now arrived at the Mesozoic deposits. After fully rehydrating, you dig in again.

You pass an envelope full of school Boxtops for Education that you never turned in; a stack of receipts, neatly paper-clipped together, from Christmas 2005; warranties that have just expired for appliances that have just broken; a once-considered state-of-the-art travel alarm clock; a tiny box of wax strips for your daughter's braces; and a clip-on bowtie.

You find earbuds in cases, earbuds out of cases, empty cases where earbuds used to be—until you reach, at the bottom of the drawer, the time before earbuds even existed in your house (let's call it "B.E."), where there lies a black foam disk that once covered the earpiece to a headset, and a half-burnt candle in the shape of a 1.

And you are stunned to realize that you have lived there this long and that enough time has passed for children to have become fully grown and for extraordinary and life-changing inventions to have occurred in the world since you moved in.

Time has a funny way of warping and folding over onto itself again. I have a rule of thumb regarding time; I estimate how long ago I think something happened, and then I multiply that by three. Because however long ago I think something happened, it actually took place far longer ago than that.

But digging through the drawer inverts that rule. Those things you unearthed that are now scattered all over the kitchen counter—they came from last week, last year, last decade. They are from a time that was both yesterday and a lifetime ago. Somehow, it's all the same.

And then you view your little junk drawer as what it really is: a time-capsule of your family.

So you pause, and then you put it all back again.

16 ON KEATS AND POLLEN

While at Trader Joe's last week, I stopped to admire the display of flowers that were stationed outside the door, and I was successfully won over by the daffodils. I peered into the collection and pulled out a few pots, assessing their size and the proportion of blossoms-to-buds, when a fellow shopper passed by.

"Make yourself happy," she said to me as she entered the store.

She nailed it.

That's exactly why I was buying the flowers.

Imparting happiness, injecting our world with buoyancy—that's what flowers are for.

Flowers are something like smiles. They are fleeting, but they brighten the world and lighten the spirit. They are gracious and elegant, yet attainable and commonplace. They smack of indulgence, yet they are natural and gluten-free.

During springtime in Atlanta, we are surrounded by floral smiles. Our fluffy cherry trees, our feathery dogwoods, our brilliant azaleas are smiling at us from all sides, causing us to smile in return.

And sneeze. They cause us to smile and sneeze and itch and dab our watery eyes. Don't think I would fail to mention that.

But back to the flowers.

They also remind me of that famous line by John Keats (I looked it up), "A thing of beauty is a joy forever: its loveliness increases; it will never pass into nothingness…"

Well, you and I know that unless it's laminated or made of some form of stone, a thing doesn't physically last forever. Flowers certainly don't. I love irises, love their double triumvirate of petals—one set arching skyward and one bowing gracefully toward the earth—but when cut, they are the mayfly of flowers, in that they die in about a day.

Still, I love them. I love both the sight of them and the memory of them.

Not meaning to launch into a dissertation on Keats, but rather to confine this poetic moment to a single paragraph more, I will admit that Keats was right there with me. He was not intending to laminate beautiful things; rather, he was rhapsodizing about nature as well as the pleasant remembrance of things that naturally die, "but will still keep a bower quiet for us, and a sleep full of sweet dreams, and health, and quiet breathing."

Obviously, though, Keats didn't live in Atlanta, where all these things of beauty spew storms of ghastly yellow pollen that keep us sniffling and wheezing. There is no "quiet breathing" during spring in Atlanta, while we are gazing at our things of beauty. And that reminds me of another beauty-themed idiom, which is that beauty comes at a price.

Thus in my column for today, we have Keats on beauty, and pollen on flowers, and smiles on faces, and springtime in Atlanta. And I am going to attempt to tie all of these themes into a neat little bow and close by coining a phrase of my own: "A smile carries no pollen."

So this spring, plant flowers if it makes you happy. And smile.

17 A WINK AND A SMILE

*I*n an effort to demonstrate our range of human emotions and yet still move beyond the constraints of basic punctuation and a shrunken vocabulary, we, as a technically evolved culture, have dawdled across our keyboards and touch pads and discovered an abundance of ways to form a smiley face.

I'm constantly amazed at the variety.

Even though there are myriad variations on your average smartphone—ranging from a blushing grin to a sassy wink to a nostril flaring devil to a cry-me-a-river—

there are those of us who won't succumb to prepackaged emoticons and prefer to inject our own creations into our correspondences. There are others of us who take into account the coolness factor and, in so doing, shun the ready-mades altogether.

And of course, there are those who compose actual emails on actual laptops, and thus have the full keyboard at their disposal at all times and who have experimented with all the emotional combinations available, creating their own emoticons out of punctuation marks and using what I will call "puncticons."

I know you've seen puncticons, and I'll bet you've used a few yourself. Like clothing and hairstyle, your puncticon choices reveal something of your personality. If you are like my son, for instance (who can wring more emotion out of a keypad than anyone I've ever met), you are not just happy, you're filled with wide-eyed exuberance =D!, sometimes unsure =d, and sometimes upside down with glee (=.

If you are like my daughter, who is perennially cheerful and cute, you will have fittingly cheerful and cute puncticons, so that when you're happy, you're happy cute :D, and even when you're bummed, you're bummed cute :/. Most of us like to save time by foregoing the "shift" and "space" keys and end up being squishy cute ;).

Usually I don't hit the shift key fast enough, and my

faces are filled with nines or underscores :9 ;9 ;_9, which looks a bit piggish and which I doubt will catch-on.

My biggest problem comes when I insert a puncticon into a parenthetical phrase (which I often do), and then I end up making a happy face with a double-chin (and it's somewhat confusing :)).

I decided to experiment with the happy-face theme myself, punching keys to see what shapes they'd make and feeling like a kid with a new box of crayons who's curious about just what color "sienna" turns out to be. I started by taking the time to give my face a nose :-) but my laptop no longer allows manually created happiness and interjects its own ☺.

I put it on html so that I could dress my little face and give him hair }:-) or a mustache :{D for added character. I made Goldilocks with a dollar sign $:D, I made a happy guy with a big nose {: >), and I made an alien (-)

Then I tried to come up with my own personalized happy face, and, since my eyes get all squinty when I smile, I came up with an inferred-joy face ^^. If I want to make a mouth, I'll have to go to an entirely new line.

^^

O

Note that with this choice, I can be nothing but surprised.

I will admit that it's a bit silly, a bit sophomoric, but

the truth is that all of these electronically composed faces are made in an effort to soften—and even humanize—the fast-paced correspondence of our times.

And I do find it heartening that even amid our busy lives and our technological haste, we will still take the time for a wink and a smile.

18 EXTREME FOOD

hen my first child was but a toddler, his favorite show was a cooking show. It featured reruns of a genteel and tie-clad Graham Kerr charmingly slicing, dicing, and "nice-ing" his way around his kitchen. My son loved to cuddle up next to me while we watched "the cooking man" together, presumably because my boy was so captivated by a person who did more in a kitchen than sprinkle Cheerios on a highchair tray.

Since then, the world of cooking shows has exploded, and I mean that literally. We have an entire network devoted to food and its preparation, and it's been turned into a prime-time battle. Other networks have taken notice and are getting in on the food-fight; now our TV shows are like middle school cafeterias gone wild.

We might watch the Barefoot Contessa calmly create a ganache during the sunny daytime hours, but when the sun sets, we're ready for some action. So network producers are finding ways to make even the tamest of subjects...*extreme*. Simply put, we'll watch a cupcake if it's made to look like a tank.

Chefs are chopped! Kitchens are cutthroat! Brussels sprouts battle broccoli spears. Chef Bobby Flay is in a boxing ring, and cooking contestants are dressed as gladiators. It's not enough to help someone remake his restaurant—it has to be *impossible*! Bash a sledgehammer to it, set it on fire, or link it to the mob, and we'll take notice. And yes, the innocent cupcake—a food that is synonymous with "harmless"—has been turned into a war.

I caught an episode of *Hell's Kitchen* one night. It was on during a rare evening when everyone in my family was gone, so I had the house to myself and could settle down on the couch in front of the tube with a bowl of cereal and the remote control. At first, I had no idea what I was watching; I never knew there could be such intensity in a kitchen that didn't involve three kids who were late to a soccer game. The program features Gordon Ramsay—a blonde, blue-eyed chef with a foreign accent and a foul mouth. He out-cooks and out-cusses everyone. The background music sounds like the score of a fifty-year-old WWII movie, and chefs dash around as if they're preforming triage while Ramsay shouts riveting dialogue such as "Season it! Season it! Quick! Get-The-Kale! The *bleeping* chicken is RAW!"

It was strangely compelling, like watching a wrecking ball demolish a building.

Then a commercial came on, so I clicked the remote and found *Mystery Diners*, a program whose purpose is to uncover kitchen criminals. An "investigative team" had placed hidden cameras all over a restaurant, and the restaurant owner and the head investigator were sitting in a private room, watching as employees accepted bribes and pilfered bags of flour. It wasn't exactly dinner with the Corleones…frankly, it looked pretty staged. But, like an unbalanced checkbook, it was oddly intriguing.

Okay, that one I watched for a while. But only because I really wanted to know who was stealing the beer kegs.

And then I flipped back to *Hell's Kitchen*—but only because I wanted to see if the red bandanas were going to beat the blue bandanas in the Guess the Protein challenge. (The blue team won.)

I clicked over to the Food Network again. *Cutthroat Kitchen* had just started, featuring Alton Brown trying to look sinister. Okay, I watched that for a while…but only because I wanted to see if the Italian guy could cook macaroni and cheese in a metal pipe.

A commercial came on and I hit the remote again. I clicked past thirty different crime shows that were half over and an airing of *Texas Chainsaw Massacre*.

So I clicked back to the Food Network. It was pretty tame in comparison.

And the Italian guy won.

19 IRON CHEF MOM

*T*think that many of us, while browsing through 185 channels trying to find thirty minutes of mindless entertainment, once discovered the program *Iron Chef* or one of its many children and lingered there for a few moments.

The premise of *Iron Chef America* was enticing: a Master Chef, usually someone who is renowned for the cuisine at his or her restaurant, was pitted against one of the Food Network's own "Iron Chefs." Each chef had two helpers, along with all of the food and technology that Kitchen Stadium could provide, and were charged with creating (within the hour) six gourmet courses that featured a Secret Ingredient.

Competition was overseen by The Chairman, who acrobated himself onto stage, swooshed his head, and said hello. Then, using a good deal of aplomb, he revealed said Secret Ingredient and set the contestants scurrying with the words "Allez Cuisine!"

I must say that I was pretty impressed with that Iron Chef program. How could I not be? There were teams of sous chefs who could dice a pound of onions in less time than it takes me to find my cutting board. There were chefs who could produce—and gorgeously plate—six dishes in roughly the same amount of time it takes me to microwave a package of chicken enchiladas.

But I grew a little weary of watching a competition that revolves around the meals that two super chefs can make from a reindeer. I want to see television start featuring a *real* challenge. I want to see an Iron Chef Mom.

We all have our Iron Chef Mom moments. You're in the kitchen with one child who's late for soccer practice, one who needs help with some "new math" homework, and a two-year-old who needs a diaper change, when the tiny Chairman Voice in your head asks, "What can you make with...*a bag of frozen ravioli and a can of refried beans!?*"

I want to see a competition that celebrates our everyday Home Kitchen challenges. Home Kitchen Stadium would have a counter full of mail, a table piled with laundry, and a dog. The Chairman would be the Original Iron Chef's Mother-in-Law. Prizes are a month's supply of lasagna and a spa weekend. A chef wins if her kids eat her food.

Alton Brown can still be the commentator. (We like him). His commentary would sound something like this:

"Our Iron Chef Mom is a veteran mother of two whose crowning achievement was making veal parmesan for twenty while her house was being painted and her daughter was going through a breakup with her boyfriend.

"Our challenger is a worthy opponent whose cookbook, *365 Ways to Use Cream of Chicken Soup*, is a best seller and whose three-year-old twins are at this moment smearing the walls of Home Kitchen Stadium with garlic paste.

"Tonight, we're going to see if they can make dinner out of...*a jar of anchovies and an old cucumber!*"

"You'd better hurry!" says Chairman Mother-in-Law.

"And they're off!

"The challenger runs to the supplies and grabs a stack of *Dora the Explorer* DVDs to buy her three minutes of prep time.

"On the home side, Iron Chef Mom is making burritos out of our Secret Ingredients and a can of Vienna sausages while fielding a phone call from her daughter, whose car battery died in the middle of the left-turn lane out of the high school parking lot.

"Meanwhile, the challenger has combined those anchovies with her trademark cream of chicken soup and poured it over animal-shaped pasta. Her twins have been tormenting Home Kitchen Dog, so she's…letting them take turns with the cucumber and the juicing machine. Brilliant.

"Iron Chef Mom has told her daughter that the jumper cables are under the baseball gloves in the trunk and is talking her through how to jump the car (that's what makes her Iron, folks!) while plating the burritos for her son and three of his friends, who have just entered Home Kitchen Stadium looking for something to eat.

"Now for the test…Will They Eat It?

"Yes! The boys ate the burritos!

"Oh no…on the challenger's side, the twins spit out their food! But wait…the dog is eating it, so our challenger still gets the lasagna! Here at Home Kitchen Stadium, everyone's a winner, just like Mom says!

"So until next week, we leave you with final words from Chairman Mother-in-Law:"

"What's in YOUR freezer?"

20 APPARENTLY, WE HAVE DIFFERENT PARENTING STYLES

People love to complain about their kids, but if you raise them right, they can be great assets. They'll babysit each other. They'll take out the trash. They'll open a bottle of wine for you and pour you a hefty glassful while you're reheating dinner.

It all comes down to your parenting style and your parental goals. Me? I raised my kids to sleep late and appreciate good comedy.

I started them young. If they awakened before dawn, I'd pull them back into bed with me and whisper into their tiny, infantile ears, "Sleep is good…sleep is good." They didn't know that 7 a.m. existed until they started kindergarten.

I nursed my babies while watching Dave Letterman, Conan O'Brian, and reruns of *Seinfeld*, so they learned to laugh while latching-on. As they aged into coherence, I tutored them with the classics. I'd gather them around the laptop to show them YouTube videos of Eddie Murphy's Hot Tub and Dan Aykroyd's Bassomatic, saying, "Look, kids! This is what we watched before there were reality shows!"

Let's face it, we all have different parenting styles. "Experts" try to classify them into a few distinct types— authoritative, permissive, *laissez-faire*, for example. But I think we're all really parenting combination-plates. For instance, I've identified my own parenting style as *laissez-authoritarian-it's-not-faire*.

It's a style that's been working for me. By the time my kids were in middle school, I could use my cellphone to call them from my bed and ask them to empty the dishwasher…and then come upstairs to kiss me goodbye before they left for the bus stop.

Problems arise, however, when houseguests have a different parenting style.

My most scarring experience came when my children were very young and an old friend of mine stayed with us for a week. She and I used to dance on tables together, back in our single days. She used to drink cosmopolitans, and she looked great in a mini-skirt. She was all about fun.

So imagine my surprise when, years later, she came to visit with her own children and a strict authoritarian attitude. Eager to set boundaries for her offspring, she asked me for my House Rules. I didn't have a list at the ready, so I thought I'd make something up.

"Well," I started jokingly, "I don't let them run naked through the living room."

Right on cue—I kid you not—my little boy ran naked through the living room.

I don't think I have to tell you that I felt like a fool and a failure, and the visit went downhill from there.

After that (rather humiliating) experience, I questioned my own child-rearing techniques. Was I too permissive or too controlling? Was my son running around naked because I was too lenient? Or was he rebelling against too-strict expectations? Or was romping about *alfresco* just a fun thing to do?

I've since accepted the fact that our parenting styles, like our families, are as individual as snowflakes or tastes in music.

I might have felt like an incompetent parent when I was raising toddlers, but I'm not concerned any more...

because my kids let me sleep late, they like Steve Martin, and right now they're mowing the lawn.

21   THE YOGA CLASS

I started taking yoga because I am running out of exercises that don't hurt my knees, shoulders, lower back, hips, or head. Besides that, at the end of a yoga class we all lie peacefully on our mats in the darkened room while meditative sitar music plays, and the only other way I can justify lying flat on my back for five minutes in the middle of the day is if I'm getting an MRI.

Now, I'll tell you straight away that yoga is sort of a sadistic version of "Simon Says." The yoga instructor will lead you through a series of poses that I am convinced the human body was never designed to make. The underlying theory of the practice is that you can purify your mind and body and become one with the universe by pretending that you're a contortionist.

But the great thing about yoga is that even if you can't do all the positions, most of rest of the people in the class can't, either. There will always be one, however, who will make all of the poses perfectly. She will wrap her knees around her ears, balance her entire body on her knuckles, and then touch her tongue to her nose besides, just to make the rest of us feel worse about ourselves.

But don't mind her. Watch me.

Classes often center on a series of poses called the Sun Salutation, and they are basically like a highly advanced game of "Head, Shoulders, Knees, and Toes." It is very hard to do once you have passed adolescence.

Yoga teachers like to talk about your "prana"—an invisible ball of energy that forms in the space between your hands. Its cousins are Harvey the Rabbit and Casper the Friendly Ghost. Sometimes the class will divide into teams and throw their pranas across the room for an invisible game of catch, and sometime everyone will hold their invisible balls in place and wait for Godot.

In a yoga class, the instructor will lead the class through the poses by naming them either in the traditional Sanskrit or their English translations, which creates an odd combination of 1) words that you've never heard before but that still sound oddly familiar and 2) names of common animate and inanimate objects. For instance, Chaturanga Dandasana and Uttanasana will be interspersed with Happy Baby, Angry Cat, Table Top, and a whole series of Warriors.

So a typical class will go like something like this:

"Good morning, class. Let's start on our mats in the Jujubeansarana pose...breathe....feel the breath and set your intention for today's practice.

"Good. Now slowly move—knees, chest and chin—into Dead Donkey. Hold it. Listen to what your body is telling you. Raise the right leg....bend it to the side and open up the hips...we're in Vanmorrisonishina... moving into Ticked-Off Teenage Daughter.

"Now straighten the right leg, still holding it behind you...wrap your arms behind your back and grab your wrists...turn towards the wall and feel the twist...we're in Ottomanempire. Move back to center...Now gradually lift the left leg, while lowering down to balance on your head. Hold the pose....Remember to breathe. Now slowly unwrap your arms and position your hands on either side of your ears...make sure they're lined up properly...and rise up into Flying Whoopee Cushion.

"Beautiful.

"Okay, lower back to Nadiacomaneciana, with chest,

chin, and palms on your mat. Be careful not to poke yourself in your Third Eye. We're going to go into Left-Over Meatloaf...envision yourself in this pose before we move into it. Very good.

"Roll over to your side and slowly push up into a sitting position, and let's end the class with a few cleansing breaths. Breathe in and hold for a count of five, now blow out all at once and make a sound like a lion giving birth...ROAHHHAAAAH!! Good.

"Let's do that three more times. Gradually raise your arms parallel to the ground. Bring your right hand slowly to your mouth. Pop an Altoid.

"Now close your eyes, palms to chest."

Namaste.

22 GOING BANG BUSTERS

hile at the gym last week, I heard two women talking about a Fringe Fighter. I thought that they were referring to another Marvel comics super-hero; I figured that maybe the Fringe Fighters movie would premier sometime between *The Avengers* and *Justice League*.

But no, they were talking about a headband.

This I should have known, since I, myself, own a Bang Buster. The Bang Buster isn't just any headband; it is "performance gear" headwear, a designer piece of thick reversible material that is worn across the forehead and enables today's female athlete to power through any workout without the threat of hair falling in her face. It's strong, it's sassy, it's stylish.

When I wear it, however, I look like an Arapahoe hippie.

It seems that as our exercise habits have evolved, so has the world of athletic garb. These days, we make a fashion statement when we sweat. For one thing, the days of cotton T-shirts and baggy shorts are long gone—modern-day gym wear is way more complicated than that. Today's athletic tops are Rubik's Cubes with armholes. Sports bras are sewn into sheer, flowy racer-back tanks, and putting one on is like climbing into an Escher print. And that's discouraging, because if I'm not fit enough to get in and out of the work-out clothes, how is my actual work-out going to go? Running shirts are made using unstinkable technology, and they breathe and wick away sweat. Basically, my gym clothes work harder than I do.

Still, my work-out wardrobe could use a little update, as even my Bang Buster has been discontinued. So I went online to search for a pair of shorts (while eating a bowlful of ice cream) and became immediately demoralized.

I decided that I needed to set a few game rules regarding the performance gear I was browsing:

1. If the model wearing it has a tattoo, it will not fit

me.

2. If she has a navel piercing, I need to go to a different website.

3. If she's doing a sideways split while balancing on one hand, I refuse to buy from that company, based on principle alone.

I scrolled past a pair of leggings that looked like they belonged in the Bodies exhibit, and I scrolled past everything camo. I found some "sonar shorties" that looked truly stunning on the model, and after a few fanciful moments imagining that they would look that good on me, reality set in and I realized that they would have the dual effect of creating both muffin top and muffin thighs at the same time. It would be like squeezing the middle of a toothpaste tube.

And that's just it: You've already got to look a certain way before you'll drop $128.95 on a piece of neon green Spandex. And if you do look that way, you drop the cash because those are the rules. If you're the queen of England, you wear the tiara; if you've got the body, you wear the crop top.

Those ads showing three women on safari in yoga gear are not geared for the novices among us—they are for those who have advanced to waif wear. Starter workout clothes are made of velour or nylon, and they cover the navel. There is nothing sexy about them, and we like it that way.

All of this is to say that I think I've plateaued at headbands.

23 MAY DAY! MAY DAY!

   very couple of years, one of our kids graduates from some level of higher learning, so I clean the house and throw a party.

We also use a graduation as an excuse to make some home improvements. So, for one weekend every few years, our house looks great.

With our first graduation, we built a deck. With the second one, we landscaped the yard. We had another graduation this spring, which was perfect timing, because the windows needed cleaning.

This time around, though, we were going to keep the

party simple—just cake, coffee, and congratulatory conversation on a Sunday afternoon. It would be (pardon
the pun) a piece of cake. But just as I have forgotten the
pains of childbirth, I forgot about the pains of having a
party at home…so there I was this May, laboring once
again to get the house and yard ready.

I began preparations two weeks before the party; like
a good Southern woman, I started by planting flowers.
I bought planters, trellises, and an assortment of flora.
I also stocked-up on hydrangeas, because nothing says
Southern hospitality like hydrangeas.

Then I moved to the inside of the house and cleaned
until the place was unrecognizable. I vacuumed curtains,
I defrosted the freezer, I dusted the logs in the fireplace.
I banished textbooks from the kitchen table and moved
files to the basement where they would languish next to
the five boxes of miscellaneous items collected before our
last party.

We were only inviting family members and a few
neighbors, and I told my daughter she could invite as
many friends as she wanted. I figured we might have a
total of about forty people. The weekend before the party, Daughter emailed me from her dorm room with the
message, "Hee hee, it turns out that I have more friends
than I thought. Can I invite sixty?"

Sure honey. Bring 'em on. I had ten planters of new

flowers on the deck, anyway.

But with an ENA (estimated number of arrivals) ranging from sixty-five to ninety, I needed to recalculate the food and beverage supply. I was not raised with a less-is-more mentality; my mother taught me instead that more is probably not enough. It was time to delegate and go to Costco. My mother volunteered for duty, so I made her Brigadier General of brownies.

It was "Party" minus three days and counting. Refrigerators were stocked, floors were shined. Photos, platters, and beverage dispensers were at their stations. My husband was coming to the dinner table with his leaf-blower still strapped on. At P minus 2 days, my boys were not allowed into the house with their shoes on, and at P minus 1, they were not allowed inside at all.

All that remained were the last-minute preparations.

At 0900 hours on P-Day, I was on my hands and knees wiping dried coffee stains off of my kitchen cabinets. My son saw me and said, "Is that really necessary?"

"The devil is in the details, honey," I replied.

At P minus 2 hours, I started shouting orders like a sergeant preparing for an invasion:

"You! Put ice in the coolers!"

"You! Unpack the croissants!"

"You! Tie balloons to the flower pots by the front door!"

Then reinforcements landed. My mother entered the house with seven dozen brownies, my sister had four back-up gallons of lemonade, and my cousin mobilized the fruit and cheese trays. Yes, only cake and coffee were advertised, but who was I kidding? We had enough to feed Bulgaria.

Friends and family arrived, and our graduate came home, along with eds and co-eds. They came, they ate, they conquered. It was a terrific party. It lasted only a few short hours, but the aftermath lingers: my potted plants are still flourishing and the windows are pollen-free.

Will I do this again? Of course I will—I've got two more that will graduate high school in a few years. Actually I can hardly wait, because the house needs painting.

24 WE CARRY OUR CHILDREN

I carried them to term, thirty-eight weeks. They were 6.5 lbs. and 6.7 lbs. and each measured 19 1/2 inches, a remarkable dual heft for a 5 foot,1 inch me.

I carried them, hip on hip, side to side, front and back, for the first year. I carried them one at a time—on a Boppy Pillow in my lap and draped across my shoulder. I carried them in tandem—strapped into strollers and car seats, in a backpack, and in a front sling. I carried them through colicky days and feverish nights, through Chuck E. Cheese bouncy-ball pits and Chick-fil-A slides.

I shuttled them to school, karate lessons, swim meets, soccer practice, baseball games, campouts, and Scout meetings. I hauled them to shoe shopping and suit fittings and countless times to REI. I drove them to doctors' offices and school dances, to birthday party days and movie meet-up nights.

I drove them to airports for departure to grandparent vacations and summer adventures.

I carried them to college visits and spring breaks and school dance picture parties.

This month, as I watch my twin boys carry their high school diplomas across the stage, I will continue to feel their weight in my arms.

They may not know it, they may not like it, but they are a part of me and I carry them with me as completely and naturally as I carry my own heart.

And after graduation, I will carry them still.

We all carry our children. They are there in our minds and our guts, our hopes and our fears. We carry them through sickness, disappointments, and breakups. When they don't make the team, when their friends move away, we feel the loss and we share in the sadness. We carry them through health, accomplishments, and satisfaction. When their team wins, when they made the cut, we feel the elation and we share in the thrill. And through all the ups and downs, we carry them...with love and prayer and wringing hands and gleeful hugs.

We teach them to stand and to walk and to be independent; raising self-sufficient adults is, after all, our ultimate goal. (And yes, you can throw in "happy," "well-adjusted," "contributing member of society," and any number of enriching adjectives, but you get my point). Yet our children are irrevocably connected to us through the bonds of parenthood, and it is within those parental bonds that we carry them.

We carry them with joy and pride and utter astonishment that these beings grew up before our very eyes and developed into strong and capable adults.

We will carry them still, through dorm move-in day and college football games, through interviews and job searches, through engagements and weddings and births, through new lives and new dreams and new families emerging.

It is the way of the world. Once we carry our tiny miracles as helpless infants, they become ours, and we carry them with us, forever.

SUMMER

25 COME FLY WITH ME

I't's finally time! It's time to hop on a plane and take that getaway you've been waiting for all year.

You've worked hard, you've chosen your destination, planned your itinerary, and purchased your tickets.

You have shrink-wrapped all your clothes and crammed them and your essentials into a 9"x 14"x 22" carry-on bag, so that you won't be charged an extra twenty-five bucks each way for luggage and so that your bag will be stored reassuringly above your own head and you won't run the risk of checking it and having it wind up in Bogota, Colombia, (which has happened).

You have parked your car in Row 64-G of the Wherez-My-Car lot, and you have stashed your ticket in a very special place that you will completely forget a week from now.

You have snaked through a security line so long that you became briefly comatose and then finally awoke expecting to see Splash Mountain in front of you.

You have escalated down and up and side to side and walked and trammed and shuttled and people-moved to your terminal.

You have found your gate and settled yourself between a teenager who is working his way through the jumbo bag of fried onion rings and a sleeping woman who is flying stand-by and has been there since last Tuesday.

At last, it's time to board!

You listen as the gate agent announces that the crew is now ready for "pre-board," which allows mothers additional time to get on the plane with their young children who all happen to have ear infections. (I was once one of those moms).

You check your ticket and wait your turn. Now the gate agent is calling for their Premium boarding: "All our Diamond members, Medallion members, Pendant members, Ornament members, Olympians, Super-Duper-Special-Elite Club members, Nobel Prize Winners, and Poet Laureates may board."

That's not you. You watch the crowd file onto the jet bridge while an even larger crowd gathers, expectantly.

"It's now time for Priority boarding. Our Platinum members and Gold members, our Comfort level, Cushy level, Posh level, and also our Virgin Lithuanian Fly Club members, please come to the agent, with your tickets in hand."

Moments pass.

"Zone One may now board. That's Silver, Silver medallion, Blue Silver, Flying Silver, Hi-Ho Silver, Corporate Silver, and High Achievers."

Still not you.

"Zone Two may now board. Nickel, Copper, Zinc, Aluminum, Magnesium, Germanium, Plebeians, and the Red Birds and Blue Birds reading groups."

There's only one zone left, and it's got to be yours.

"Zone Three. Gallium, Boron, Silicon, and the rest of the Periodic Table may now board, plus Paper and Wood.

"There is no more room in the overhead compartment for your carryon bags, Zone Three, but we will check them for you for your convenience. We assure you that, although you will not find them in baggage claim at your destination, they will safely arrive in Bogota, Colombia.

"We hope you enjoy your flight."

And so your trip begins. Let's hope the rest of your vacation is first class.

26 WE'VE BEEN SICK IN ALL THE BEST PLACES

hen you have four kids, odds are that in any given month one of them will get sick. In fact, the folks at my local pharmacy know me by the sound of my voice, which is nice in a small-town-friendly sort of way, but at the same time a bit unsettling.

When you are about to embark on a family vacation, however, the odds of illness increase because you must factor in Murphy's Law (ML), which states that whenever something can go wrong, it will, and which results in the following equation:

$$\frac{4(\text{urgent care}) \times 52ML^2}{\$(\text{HSA})} = \frac{Rx(\text{length of illness})}{3y(\text{length of vacation})}$$

Thus you see that the result is roughly an 89 percent probability that at least one child will become sick or have a medical emergency within three days of the vacation, with the duration and severity of the condition in direct inverse proportion to the amount in your health savings account. The longer your trip, the higher the risk factor, so that if you are gone for more than one weekend, illness or injury is inevitable.

The upshot is that we've been sick in all the best places.

I prepare for the inevitable by always packing a first aid kit, including everything from echinacea and Benadryl to moleskin and crutches. I also employ the popular new-age method of positive thinking: "You're fine...Now *run!*"

A few years ago, we took an epic two-week family minivan adventure-trip to Niagara Falls and back down the East Coast. (Two weeks in the minivan! You can imagine how excited I was when my husband suggested this particular vacation, since driving around in a minivan full of kids is something I really don't do enough.)

We were traveling from Atlanta to Nashville to Upstate New York for the first few legs of the journey. I had a first aid bag the size of my body that was filled with lozenges, pills, drops, slings, and a snake-bite kit, and naturally, on evening three of our trip—a Sunday, of course—my daughter complained that her eye hurt.

As I dropped some Visine into her right eye we looked at each other, knowing that there was nothing in my arsenal to ward off whatever she had.

She woke up the next morning with her eye swollen shut. I called our eye doctor, who called in a prescription for antibiotic drops, which we filled and then loaded ourselves into the car. When my daughter pried her eye open enough for me to instill the drops, however, I saw a disturbing yellowish goo distending from her cornea, and I called the doctor again. He grew extremely concerned and said that we needed to go to an ophthalmologist immediately and get her eye cultured. His entire staff kicked into gear. They located an ophthalmologist on our route, called his office, and informed him of the situation.

We were south of the Sweet Tea Line, which lies just beyond the Mason-Dixon, driving through Kentucky in search of the ophthalmologist. We made it to his office before closing time and ran the culture to the hospital across the street. My daughter was being tested for a cornea-eating bacteria.

Every hour on the hour, through Ohio, New York, and into Canada, I leaned across the minivan seats to instill more drops into my daughter's eyes. I got the call from the Kentucky ophthalmologist a few days later, while I was standing in a poncho on the Maid of the Mist; my girl had indeed contracted the dreaded bacteria. We continued our journey back down the Eastern seaboard, stopping for hamburgers and ophthalmologist checkups all along the way.

The bacteria did eat a tiny hole into my daughter's cornea, just a tiny one, and I thank God, modern medicine, my eye doctor, and every ophthalmologist from here to Niagara Falls that my daughter's vision is intact today.

So to all of you families out there, traveling on family vacation, have a safe and healthy trip!

And I'll see you at the doctor's office.

27

DIE, CHIP AND DALE, DIE!

The sign at the entrance of our neighborhood warns, in large letters, "COYOTES in the Neighborhood! Guard Your Pets!"

When my husband read that he said, "Maybe they'll eat the chipmunks."

If only.

I, too, have grown to be a chipmunk hater.

For years, I thought they were cute and loveable. When I was a child, I enjoyed watching them in their animated forms being zany with all the other talking cartoon creatures of Saturday morning. I loved them and their striped-fur appeal throughout my adolescence and into the stages of my early adulthood.

I was charmed by them, still, when we met, person-to-chipmunk, at Disneyworld. We had taken our two young, impressionable tots to the Minnie-Ha-Ha-Menehune–Make-Me-Say-Things-I-Can't-Believe-I'm–Saying Character Breakfast at the Polynesian Villages Restaurant.

Chip and Dale were headliners then, along with Minnie Mouse in a grass skirt, and we were keen to meet the pair of chipmunks—terrifyingly large and plastic-eyed, though they were. We hugged their gigantic, faux-fur bodies, got their autographs, and even joined the conga line with them. They congaed like nobody's business. We learned that we could tell the two of them apart because Chip has the "chocolate chip nose."

Well, it's all over, rodent. I'm a homeowner and a gardener now, and that piece of cocoa on your face is not going to save you.

These tiny, scampering little furballs may appear adorable and harmless, but in reality, they are treacherous. They tunnel under brick and concrete, creating structural havoc. They chew through wires and tulip bulbs, and they raid gardens and eat vegetables that are meant for humans, not disease-carrying varmints. They can ingest thirty-seven dollars' worth of pansies, overnight.

Someone told me that cayenne pepper is a good natural repellant for chipmunks. I did try it, emptying three bottles in the holes under my front porch. But really, that's like trying to hold a wolf at bay with a cigarette lighter.

For years I watched these destructive, disdainful critters scurry in and out of my flowerbeds, impervious to neighborhood dogs, hawks, snakes, and spice jars. I finally decided that it was time to call in the big guns, and I enlisted the help of the professionals.

I googled "kill the rodents" until I found a professional near me. A man from the Chipmunk Patrol drove up to my house the next day and determined that I did have an infestation.

An infestation! I had just been calling it a nuisance! But now my problem was being defined by a term that was making my skin crawl. This was serious.

The Chipmunk Patroller said that he could trap the rodents and remove them, and that sounded like a good plan to me at first. The (excuse me) "catch" was that the company used live traps, which meant that once trapped, the disgusting creatures could theoretically languish there, alive and wriggling, until the Chipmunk Patroller came to remove them.

Ugh! I can't even stand the sight of an upside down cockroach.

Then the professional rodent destroyer told me that if the burrows were deep enough, he could drop smoke bombs in there—lethal to the chipmunks, but harmless to children, birds, and pets.

Perfect. Die, Chip and Dale, Die!

So Mr. Chipmunk dropped the smoke bombs, and for exactly two weeks I could watch our garage door open without seeing a gang of chipmunks scatter like thugs being raided at a craps game.

Then they all found their way into my tomatoes and under my deck again.

I'm going to put up a sign of my own, in my front yard. It will read, in large letters, "COYOTES Welcome!"

28 BIRDFEEDER BATTLES

I have a bit of a summertime routine. Each morning, as the humidity ripens and before it becomes oppressive, I go outside to my deck, drink a cup of coffee, wait for the internet to connect, drink a cup of coffee, wait for my email to update, drink a cup of coffee, try to think of something to write, drink another cup of coffee, and thus ease into my day, all the while serenaded by a cacophony of tweets and trills from the backyard birds in my backyard aviary and distracted by their flights of color.

They charm me.

I had outwitted the squirrels and chipmunks that used to shimmy over the hanging rod and squeeze *inside* the feeder; I had changed the feeder and the seed, and those pesky varmints were dining elsewhere. Since then, birds have gathered at my feeder like commuters at a Starbucks. I have been getting house finches and goldfinches, chickadees and towhees.

Sometimes I even get bluebirds, and, as we all know, bluebirds are special. Their indigo blue and cherry red colors punctuated in white and black inspire me to think of them as God's rainbow, sent to me in the form of a winged creature—a fluttering promise that everything will be okay.

The birds were happy, I was happy, life was grand. And then…and then everything went terribly wrong.

I dashed to the wild bird store and started to explain: "I was getting all kinds of songbirds—finches and cardinals, and even bluebirds, and then…"

"….and then the *grackles* came." He finished the sentence for me, and I could hear ominous music swell up in the background.

If you have a birdfeeder, you know about grackles. If you don't, I will tell you. They are large, beady-eyed, sinister-looking birds the color of old oil that travel in swarms and look as if, at any minute, they will perch on my deck railings and start cackling, "Nevermore."

I don't like them one bit.

Not only do they creep the daylights out of me, but they frighten away my pretty birds and devour my birdseed faster than it takes to say "Poe." Plus, they make a mess and they don't clean up after themselves, so they're kind of like flying teenagers.

I wanted God's winged rainbows back, not God's winged delinquents. Birdseed Man said the best thing to do was to remove the seed until the dreaded grackles went away.

So I removed the seed, and the grackles would squawk and crow and swoop by and leave their droppings all over my outdoor furniture in revenge, while my timid songbirds would hop around in forlorn curiosity, wondering what happened to their free lunch.

Finally, after the grackles tired of their retaliatory bombings and moved along, I put out the birdfeeder and the lovely red and purple and gold finches returned to charm me until the word spread through the grackle grapevine, and they came back again, in droves.

I finally appealed to the internet and discovered an entire community of bird-loving bloggers who were posting helpful suggestions under the headings "bully birds," "gangs of greedy grackles," and "unwanted birdfeeder pests." We might love birds, but there is a limit to our birdseed benevolence. The truth is, grackles are no more welcome at our feeders than rats are at an animal shelter.

One blogging birder recommended using safflower seed because grackles don't like it. So I tried that, and, lo and behold, it is working. It has the same effect of announcing to my kids that we're cleaning out the garage—it makes them disappear.

This morning I'm on my deck drinking coffee, admiring my birdfeeder that is once again covered with finches and towhees and cardinals.

And I'm waiting for bluebirds.

29 WASTE NOT, WANT NOT

T'm a "waste not, want not" type of gal. I believe I got that sensibility from my mother, who never met a scrap of wrapping paper that she couldn't line shelves with.

Whatever the reason, I've been reducing, reusing, and recycling since green was a color, not a lifestyle. I was green before it was cool, before recycling was a household word, when people like me were merely called thrifty or frugal...or cheap.

It started when I was in elementary school. I wrote assignments on both sides of my notebook paper until my teachers objected (and I was over*ruled*). Still unable to justify an unused side of paper, I now recycle my kids' schoolwork through our home printer. I've broken a $200.00 copy machine because I was using the back of an assignment that had a staple in it, but I still feel like I'm saving the planet, one reused sheet of paper at a time.

It might be noble or it might be a sickness—you decide. But I won't waste a forkful of old quinoa.

I come from a long line of green women. My mother got her sense of resourcefulness from her mother and those of The Greatest Generation whose attitudes permeated their society. They had no blue recycling bins, but that generation reused things until they were no longer recognizable.

I watched my Nana when I was young, and her approach made an impression on me. She, who grew zucchini and tomatoes and who could create something wonderful out of the gnarly quince apples from her backyard. She, who would buy a whole chicken and use every bit of it, eating the livers fried with onions and cooking the gizzards in broth, then feeding them to the dog. She, who would tear old sheets into rags and use old nylons to stuff pillows and dolls.

We've gotten away from that. We clean our homes with paper towels and we're not making sock monkeys any more. And, let's be honest—when's the last time you stuffed a pillow?

I've tried to adopt some of my Nana's ways. I boil our Thanksgiving turkey carcass to make broth—all I get is tasteless greasy water, but it's tasteless greasy water that I can feel good about. I've started growing tomatoes and zucchini. I use unmatched socks as dust rags. Like my mother, I'll reuse the same piece of tin foil until there's barely enough of it left to wrap a lemon rind.

And I have become a woman who fills her kids' plastic Easter eggs with leftover Christmas candy.

There's so much more that I could do. I could throw my abundant coffee grinds into my flower beds. I could follow Nana's example by putting inedible vegetables into my blender and using that gross liquid to fertilize plants. I could make Cream of Unwanted soup out of broccoli stalks and asparagus stems. I could peel my own carrots.

But for now I'll continue with my daily habits of green living, like saving butter wrappers to grease baking pans…and take heart in the fact that there is more in my recycle bins than there is in my trash can.

30 BLUES COUNTRY

*T*oday I'm going to explore two of the most popular musical genres of the South: country music and the blues. I'm a blues girl, myself. Now, I realize that there's a fine line between the blues and country music, and that's a line that I don't want to cross. I'll go as far as bluegrass, but I stop there.

You might say that both of these musical genres are forms of artful whining. But the difference between the blues and country music is the difference between telling it like it is and ruthlessly exploiting my emotions. If I happen to hear a country song that starts off with a letter stuck to an old oak tree, I switch the radio dial, because whoever wrote that letter is going to die. And that will make me cry. And I don't want to listen to a song and cry unless I'm watching *Les Miserables.*

With the blues, you start down and you stay down, and those minor chords make it kind of fun while you're down there. Not so with country music. You'll be Sittin' Knee-Deep in the Water Somewhere and the next thing you know, you're being showered with tears that are pouring down on you from Holes in the Floor of Heaven.

Don't jerk me around like that.

I don't want to be having a rollicking good time with my Red Solo Cup in hand and in the next moment witness my daughter growing up too quickly before my very eyes while plumbers and other sages are telling her that she's going to miss this when it's gone, which starts me spiraling straight into a Sunrise, Sunset melancholy. Stop it, already!

With the blues, I know what's coming. There will always be a minor note and a major problem, and it will be played out in a very reliable fashion. There will be a redundant chord progression, a three-line stanza, and double entendre. If I miss the first line of a verse, I don't have to worry because it'll be sung all over again—right away.

With the blues, there will be an issue with a spouse—he's either cheating or leaving. If it's a Sad, Sad Sunday, I know it's because my baby has to go. If there's nothin' I can do as you leave me here to cry, I know that my love will follow you as the years go passing by. If you been meetin' your man, baby, down at the local laundromat, then I know that someone's done got wise and daddy ain't going for that. You see? There are no surprises with this musical genre.

I respect the blues. There's integrity in them thar lyrics. It might sound real sweet to have some slick country music cowboy singing to you about how the July moonlight shines, with "your pretty little head" on his shoulder—but I've heard that line before. A blues singer will compare his woman to a whiskey store, and that sounds a whole lot more honest to me.

So give me a flatted third, a bent seventh, and predictable rhymes, and if you can't give me that, at least give me a harmonica.

I'm not trying to convert you. I know you're happy with your trucks and sunshine and cutoff jeans, your Keith Urbans and your Carrie Underwoods. But I'll take B.B. King every time.

And ain't nobody's business if I do.

31   DO OR DIET

I've tried to diet, but I'm not good at denying myself. For twenty-three years, I haven't taken a shower without someone knocking at the door with a question that can't wait another two minutes—so yes, I'm going to eat that cookie.

My mind and my body have an agreement. I dole out positive reinforcement treats to my body throughout the day, and it gets me out of bed in the morning.

There are so many theories, so many methods for dieting, and I've danced with them all and sent them home happy.

I've heard to "eat breakfast like a king, lunch like a prince, and dinner like a pauper." I pretty much eat breakfast, lunch, mid-morning snacks, and mid-afternoon happy hours like an exiled prince, and dinners like a freaking emperor. So, to use a more accurate comparison, I have the diet of a sumo wrestler. I nibble and nosh throughout the day, and I eat the heaviest, most caloric food in the last two hours before I go to bed, so that all of the calories can join hands and turn into layers of fat overnight.

I've heard to limit yourself to one sweet thing a week. I try that and end up making myself a weekly dessert the size of an Hawaiian Island.

I've heard to count calories. The problem with this method is that I am an unscrupulous cheater. I will not count the spoonfuls of ice cream that I eat, straight from the box, or the brownies that are stuck to the side of the pan that I have to pry out and consume before putting together a tray for the class party, or the melted peanut butter-chocolate power bar that I find between the minivan seats while I'm waiting in the carpool line. I only count lettuce and rice cakes. So, no matter how much I actually eat during the day, my calorie count always amounts to roughly 235.

I've heard to eat six mini-meals a day. My mini-meals turn into one constant land-cruise buffet. There might as well be an ice sculpture of a swan on my kitchen counter, right beside the uneaten fries and the container of Boy Scout popcorn.

I've heard about the Starbucks diet—that one woman lost eighty-five pounds by eating exclusively at Starbucks. I have been pretty close to doing that diet myself, but the pumpkin bread and cake pops kept winning out over the oatmeal.

The frustrating thing for me is, it wasn't always this way. Despite giving birth to four children, despite the fact that two of them were born at the same time, despite the fact that my body weight increased by half during that twins pregnancy, I always managed to return to my normal weight and jeans size and maintain it steadily.

Not true now. I have had another birthday and there are squatters at my belly. The pounds—about ten of them—have settled along my mid-section and are making plans to retire there. I don't want to take them with me when I finally, one day, become an empty nester. I want to leave them in the basement along with the boxes of kindergarten artwork.

My mother has stayed slim and trim well into her senior years, and when asked how she does it, her standard reply is "I eat whatever I want, and I never exercise."

I've tried that method too, but it doesn't seem to work as well for me. I've decided that the only thing left for me to do is follow another piece of mom's advice…to stand up straight and suck in my stomach.

32 FOOD: IT'S ALL GOOD

*I*n a perfect world, my favorite foods would have magical properties. Croissants would make my hair smooth and silky, potato chips would make me sing on key, and bacon would kill germs that cause bad breath.

Lo and behold, that world has arrived!

Every time I log on, I see a new announcement splashed across the internet that a formerly forbidden food is now considered healthy.

It started with chocolate...dark chocolate. Somewhere, somehow, someone discovered that dark chocolate is jam-packed with antioxidants, which of course are the superheroes of our generation, and furthermore, that dark chocolate releases endorphins, which are good for the soul. Chocolate with ice cream is even *better* for the soul, and if there is coconut oil somewhere in the mix, it will kill your belly fat as you eat it.

The happy news continues. Coffee is good for the muscles, red wine is good for the heart, hamburger and avocadoes are good for the brain, and beer is a probiotic. And to round things out, I will add that olive oil and garlic are good for the joints.

It's as if we've fallen into the Land of Oz. Pretty soon we'll learn that apple strudel whitens teeth and *fettuccine Alfredo* improves your chances of winning the lottery.

Why, just today, a headline appeared in the "healthy living" section of my newsfeed entitled "The Top Ten Best Foods You Can Eat." I took the bait and clicked on the link. All the usual suspects were there—blueberries, kefir, beans, spinach—but buried in the middle were *mushrooms*, which gave me pause, and then, making a grand finale appearance on the list, was pork! Pork, people, PORK! Well, now we're talking.

It appeared to me that all food is trending "good for you," so I decided to try a little experiment. I googled random foods and attached the question "Is it good for you?" And I have discovered that (with the exception of strawberries, which we've been eating *all wrong*, but that's another column), it's all good!

Guided by my original wish list, I went crazy and started with "Are croissants good for you?" I found a site which explained that, sure enough, they are! Croissants contain iron and selenium, and even though I have never in my life heard of selenium, it happens to be an essential mineral, and that is good enough for me.

And take our old friend bacon, for example. I googled "Is bacon good for you?" and up popped a post that is entirely devoted to the virtues of bacon. It's on a website called Bacon Today, posted by Boss Hog (who else) and liked by, at last count, 24,735 humans. It is titled "Top Ten Reasons Bacon is Actually HEALTHY for You!" and it informs us that bacon is good for the brain, the heart, blood pressure, general well-being, and that it can fuel your car and major industry, too.

I have spent several days researching the health benefits of foods-formerly-known-as-unhealthy. I have concluded that a hamburger cooked medium well, covered with mushrooms and melted Swiss cheese, served with a side of (gluten-free) chips, guacamole, and a beer, and finished with a dark-chocolate brownie a la mode is the ultimate brain-powering, endorphin-boosting, healthy meal.

Plus, after you eat it, you will make all the green lights.

33 THE TERRIBLE TWENTY-TWOS

I knew what to do with a two-year-old, but what do I do with a twenty-two-year-old?

By the miracle of life, the two-year-old boy who was toddling around our house—it couldn't have been twenty years ago—has suddenly become a full-grown man. He's in that nebulous area of space and time, waffling between higher education and independent living.

He's old enough to drive, vote, and serve our country, but he still doesn't know how to load a dishwasher. It's that age between learning how to cite your sources and learning how to scramble an egg.

Some say it's just a phase.

He went through phases when he was in his terrible twos. I remember that. There were books on that. There was the colicky phase, the phase of exploration, the "my little potty" phase. And although I ran myself ragged during that time, I knew that (fall-down-and-die exhaustion aside, I can't say it enough) this would *not* be the most difficult part of mothering.

He still took naps. I was still bigger than he was— and continued to be, until he turned twelve. Above all, I knew that the crap I dealt with then I could flush down the toilet.

But the age of unflushable crap has arrived.

Still, the similarities between a two-year-old and a twenty-two-year-old are remarkable.

When he was two, he waddled around the house half-naked, wearing nothing but his diapers. It was very cute. At twenty-two, he lumbers around the house, with his six foot tall, extremely hairy body, wearing nothing but boxers or a wet towel—never both at the same time. It's not so cute.

When he was two, he pattered gleefully from room to room, marking his territory with squeaky toys and sippy cups. At twenty-two, he plods from den to kitchen to bedroom, leaving a trail of stained coffee cups, half-eaten cookies, and stacks of books in his wake.

When he was two, he would wake up at three in the morning, crying from nightmares. At twenty-two, he comes *in* at three in the morning. And I'm the one having nightmares.

I remember when he was born, how I labored for twenty-six hours until he finally came into the world, how my doctor presented me with him, saying, "It's a Boy! And he's perfect!" I remember how I spent the night in the hospital, my first night as a mother, lying there with my brand new baby boy asleep on my stomach. It was the most magical night of my life.

I spoke to him as he slept in his infant oblivion. I told him about the room we had waiting for him at home, lined with stuffed animals and decorated with cheery colors. I told him about the grandparents and aunts and uncles and cousins and friends who couldn't wait to meet him or see him again. I told him that his father and I were so happy to have him, about all the things we would do together, the fun we would have.

Then my husband entered the room, ever the eager one, actually trying to give me lessons on breast feeding.

Summer break is almost over, and my son will be returning to school. I could say that I'll miss his stacks of debris and barely-clothed hairy body. But I won't. What I will miss is his company—his humor, his conversation, his incredible intelligence.

So as I close the door to his train wreck of a room, I remind myself: this is all just a phase.

34 THE SUMMER OF MY ZUCCHINI

I've always thought of zucchini as a friendly vegetable.

I suppose that's because I associate it with my Italian grandmother, who grew her own zucchini and made marvelous things with it. She baked, breaded, fried, grated, relished, and parmesan-ed it; she turned it into chocolate cake and breakfast loaves.

Thus, since I was old enough to dream of what shape my adulthood would take, I dreamed of having a garden and planting zucchini. My childhood wish was finally granted, in the form of a cleared-out piece of soil behind my mailbox, which is about the only spot in my yard that gets enough sun to support produce.

I planted tomatoes, basil, parsley, thyme, and oregano, and of course, a friendly little sprout of zucchini, and I attempted to beautify the area by fronting it with an attractive curbside camouflage of flowering annuals and perennials.

The tomatoes got pretty tall and unruly. But the *zucchini*...well the zucchini took me by surprise. What started as an innocent green sprig about the size of my pinkie soon turned my mailbox garden into *The Little Shop of Horrors*. The thick squash vines and massive green leaves stretched across the vincas in front, effectively strangling the flowers and threatening to do the same to my mailman.

Other people have attack dogs; I have an attack plant.

So, I learned that zucchini can be quite intimidating. And I learned that, unlike most living things, zucchini thrives when neglected.

My husband and I went out of town for a week and left the squash in the care of my son, who promptly neglected it, and it grew unattended to phenomenal proportions.

When my son eventually went out to water my garden, he discovered an enormous zucchini protruding from beneath the elephant-ear-like leaves of the vine. He picked it and enthusiastically texted me a photo of it, which did not come close to doing justice to the thing.

I returned home to find that single zucchini taking up the entire bottom shelf of my refrigerator. It was like a mortar shell, like a green submarine, like an Austin Mini Cooper. You could string it and use it as a cello; you could put propellers on it and fly it across the interstate; you could hollow it out and paddle it down the Chattahoochee.

It was truly a remarkable thing, most worthy of documentation. I considered mounting the stem on a wooden plaque and hanging it on my wall...because, for some reason, I took pride in its size, as if I had more to do with its uncommon monstrosity than pure inattentiveness.

I behaved like a fisherman who had finally caught "the big one." I took pictures with my zucchini. I got photos of me measuring it against my arm and against my thigh, photos of me bench pressing it and curling it.

Then I dressed up and put on mascara and got some more photos.

I have more photos with the zucchini than with my son at his graduation—probably because the zucchini wasn't complaining. But I wanted the enormity of it fully authenticated before I went in for the slaughter. So, I took one final photo of it with a measuring tape (it measured 16 inches long with a 4 inch diameter, FYI) and commenced with the cooking.

I put it in a colander in my sink and started washing it with the vegetable scrub brush, and I felt like I was bathing a small child.

I cut it in half, and then in half again, and again and again, until it was of edible portions. I only had room in my skillet for half of it—which turned out to be roughly equal to eight normally formed zucchini. I sautéed it with an also massive Vidalia onion, tomatoes, basil, parsley, oregano, and salt and pepper, and served it up with a mess of pasta, and it made a fine dinner. I gave the other half to my mother.

So, this year will forever be known in my house as the summer of my zucchini.

And I think that next year, I'll plant cucumbers.

35 FOR THE LOVE OF A SKILLET

T've decided that I've lived in the South long enough to own a skillet. And by "skillet," I mean the honest-to-goodness cast-iron variety, the likes of which Sipsey used on the Bad Guy in *Fried Green Tomatoes at the Whistle Stop Café* and Rapunzel chose as her key weapon in *Tangled*.

Once I got it and felt the heft of it, I understood: you really can kill somebody with that thing.

This is actually the second skillet I bought. I lost the first one. I had purchased a trusty Lodge brand ten-inch model in order to cook a rather enticing recipe I discovered on a blog that I followed during my blogging phase (a phase which was, like the Macarena, short-lived and unfortunate). The recipe was for cherry upside-down cake, made with corn meal, almond meal, and fresh cherries. It took two hours to make, and it was delicious.

But then I lost the skillet. And before you ask how it is possible to lose something as imposing as a cast-iron skillet, I will explain that the problem is in the storage of it. It's like figuring out where to store an anvil. I learned that it is not supposed to be stacked or covered, because that messes with its "seasoning," and that the oven is a good place to store it. Of course, the problem of what to do with it when you are actually using the oven still exists; it needs to be stashed someplace where it won't fall on your foot.

So I moved it to a corner beside the dining room table, then under the guest room bed, then in the storage room in the basement, moving deeper, ever deeper, into the recesses of our home until it lodged (heh heh) comfortably somewhere, never to be found again, unless, perhaps, by a future homeowner or an archeologist on a dig.

But our society is going retro on its road to wellness, and, thumbing my nose at Teflon, I jumped back on that train and bought another skillet.

A cast-iron skillet, however, is way more retro than Fiestaware; in fact, I don't know how far back you have to go before you've passed "retro" and landed on the prairie over an open campfire, but there I was, faced with a new skillet that was primed and ready for the seasoning, and even for something as iconic as a frying pan, I must admit that I found it a bit intimidating.

Seasoning is the process that makes the skillet somewhat cling-free. I honestly think that I never seasoned my lost skillet properly, so I decided to study up on it. I learned that there are as many opinions on the proper way to season a skillet as there are opinions on the best way to cook a Thanksgiving turkey. Everyone, from Martha Stewart to Emeril Lagasse to the guy whose wife is videotaping him in their kitchen, has an opinion.

First, you wash it—but maybe with soap or maybe you should never use soap. Then you rub it with oil—but maybe using a paper towel, or maybe you should never use a paper towel. And your oil is maybe lard, or maybe something that has never been hydrogenated, or maybe something that comes out of a tube that is specially marked "skillet seasoning oil," or maybe the absolute best seasoning oil is something like flaxseed oil and you'll have to go to a health food store to buy it and it will cost $16.99 a bottle.

Then you bake it in the oven, upside down on a foil lined pan, or not...for thirty minutes or an hour or an hour and a half...at a setting of 325⁰ or 350⁰ or 375⁰, and you leave it in there to cool for a long, long, long time because now the anvil is a burning hot piece of iron that could brand you.

Or maybe you forget the oven and do the whole thing on the stove.

And you go through this once or twice or three times, depending on time of year and what your zodiac sign is, and, most likely, how bored you are.

So I chose eclectically and added my own personal twist. I used a "dedicated rag" and coconut oil (because it burns belly fat and would make my house smell like Tahiti), and I put the pan upside down in the oven and repeated the process three times, all the while proclaiming to my family that I would not be able to cook dinner that day because I was busy seasoning my skillet.

The next day, however, we would dine on fried green tomatoes and coconut-flavored cornbread.

36 LIFE ON THE EDGE OF PASTA

I had done it. I had pushed my kids over the pasta edge. That day came last week when I asked my kids what they wanted for dinner, and one of them answered, "Nothing that rhymes with maghetti."

And I thought I was doing so well. I wasn't even using a jar of Ragu; I was making fresh tomato sauce with my own home-grown tomatoes, the noodles were Italian, the parsley hadn't gone bad, there was garlic involved...

The problem has been the summertime—that time of year when schools are out and college kids come home and the house becomes once again full of people who eat. It's the time of year when the homebound eco-system becomes skewed. The box of orange juice that used to last for a week is gone in two days, cereal is inhaled, and bananas don't even stand a chance of turning brown.

It's the time of year when my mental Rolodex of recipes gets stuck on "nothing requiring more than ten minutes of effort," and life is lived on the edge of pasta.

I mean, the kids get a summer break from school—why can't I get a summer break from cooking? So, for two out of three meals a day, I let them fend for themselves. Summertime is survival of the fittest in my house. You want to eat? Go forage for food.

Of course, I can't actually send them to the backyard to hunt rodents and eat ivy (although that would be helpful). I have to augment the food supply, and that means constant trips to the grocery store. I see the cashier at my local supermarket more than I see my own husband.

I do tend to stock our shelves with food that I like or food that I think is healthy. That creates an improbable mix, and the food pyramid in our house is a bit wonky.

At the base of the pyramid is a constant supply of ice cream (made from the milk of happy cows) and Trader Joe's dark chocolate nonpareil candies (they're high in iron). Forming the pyramid's middle are a drawer full of Vidalia onions and organic zucchini (three weeks old), several containers of Greek yogurt (plain), and humus. At the pyramid's apex are a box of rice crackers and a jar of pumpkin butter.

I did come home once with three bottles of pink lemonade, which I had purchased for a bridal shower that I was co-hostessing. As I unpacked them, one son gave them the look he usually reserves for puppies in pet-store windows and said in a pitiful voice, "I'm guessing those aren't for us, are they?"

It did the trick. I opened a bottle and poured him a glass.

But my point is that there *is* food in the house, and it flies all over me when my kids complain that there isn't.

"Mom, there's nothing to eat," they whine, circling me like the rebellious pack of hyenas from *The Lion King*.

"Yes there is, too!" I insist. "Look, there's Chia seeds! Rice cakes! Arugula!"

They stare at me, blankly.

I open the crisper in the fridge and continue, "Celery! Cream cheese! Hot dog buns!"

They perk up. "Are there any hot dogs?"

"....No."

I rummage around some more and find a package of lunch meat. "Here," I say, handing it to them. "Use this on the hot dog buns. It'll be good."

There are only a handful of days left before school begins and I'll be once again free to eat as I please, breakfasting on cappuccino and lunching on a protein bar and a head of lettuce, without worrying about the offspring. But the school year also tends to usher in a whole new kind of busy—a busy which too often dictates dinners on the fly.

So my mental Rolodex file will flip to "fast and filling." I will know it has been stuck there for too long when one of my kids finally asks what's for dinner and follows it up by saying that he wants nothing that rhymes with "nac zamboni and sneeze."

FALL

37 WE DO REAL

So I'm browsing Pinterest, trawling for inspiration, and I see it. It's just what I need to whip my family into shape. It's a "house rules" sign.

But it's not your typical "play nice," "mind your manners," and "always tell the truth" sign. It's not even a rudamentary plaque of the Ten Commandments. No. This is a house rules sign that means business.

I could tell, right off the bat, when I read the first lines:

In this house...

We Do I'm Sorrys.

We Do FUNNY!

We Do Communication.

Wow, I thought. This is a sign that doesn't let the guiding rules of our language get in the way of its point.

I wondered if its tactic would work. Maybe it doesn't matter that "I'm sorry" is already a perfectly complete sentence—maybe if it's turned into a noun and pluralized, the kids would start apologizing. Maybe that tactic would be even more effective than leading by example.

Yes, that sign got me thinking. There is brilliant appeal to the whole flippant, leave-your-grammar-at-the-doorstep approach. Somehow, it seems, if we really mess with our language, it'll make our kids feel like we're on their side, like we're all a part of a team. It's a grammatically challenged team, but we're all on it together!

I read on:

We do real.

We do Loud really well.

We do kindness. And when we're done with it, we're moving on to other virtues. (I added that last part.)

I admit, I understand the allure of the whole military talk staccato. After all, we can *be* kind and real, but if we *do* it—well, that means action, sister.

If you think about it, we can Do just about anything. We Do fifty pushups! We Do a favor! We Do our nails! We Do the laundry! We Do hard time! We Do the Hokey-Pokey!

"Do" has been our go-to helping verb since the days of Beowulf, probably, and "Do" has proven his ability to function in just about any sentence, so isn't it time to unleash him? Why not occasionally drop him between random words; why not let him function as a linking verb every once in a while?

I might even buy that sign. It'll be a lot of fun to start talking that way. I'll tell my kids to wash up and they will start whining, "But mom..."

Then I'll come back with, "No, fellas. In this house, we Do hygiene!"

And what can they say to that?

I'm going to start throwing words together and see if I will not only be understood but also sound cool enough to inspire my kids to take action:

Hey, kids! In this house...

We Are yard work!

We Have thank you!

We Do dishwasher!

Yes, that sign-maker definitely hit on something. I think we can get our families to do just about anything, if we only say it wrong.

On the other hand, I could stick with a plaque of the Ten Commandments. They're tried-and-true. They're grammatically correct with all those Thou Shalts and Thou Shalt Nots. In a way, they are the original House Rules and the precursor to all House Rules signs yet to come.

And they do cover all the bases.

They really Do.

38 MY HOME AWAY FROM HOME

I have a home away from home. I don't go there for holidays; I go there because it's part of my job. If you're a mom you know what I'm talking about. My second home is my minivan.

All the essentials of a household are contained within its automatically sliding doors. Let me show you around. First and foremost is the center of any house: the kitchen. It is located primarily in a cloth bag hanging on a hook on the back of the driver's seat, where food and beverage can be found. If we dig deep enough, we can produce a protein bar, a bag of trail mix, a half-empty water bottle, and most likely, a box of apple juice from last week's happy meal.

The utensil drawer is in the console, which contains a plastic spoon and a Swiss army knife. Thus it is possible to be gridlocked for hours and yet still have the ability to filet a trout and then open a can of fruit cocktail and eat it, too.

Adjacent to the kitchen, in a small bag on the opposite hook, is the medicine cabinet. Here we can find whatever we need for minor cuts and burns, headaches, stomach aches, sore throats, fever blisters, and bee stings...plus a can of Altoids.

If we need a tissue, nail file, or collapsible brush, we'll find it in the ladies' lounge, of which there are three—one in each row of the car. They are well-stocked with Bert's Bee's Lip Shimmer, tubes of mascara, baby powder, an assortment of magazines, and some moist towelettes.

The basement is in the rear of the van, where we have a Yoga mat and exercise bands. There is also a rogue golf ball that has been rolling around the car for the last four months, and if you find that, please give it to me.

The mudroom is conveniently located immediately inside the passenger door and holds two umbrellas (one folding, one broken), a rain hat, sunglasses, my walking shoes, and one dirty sock belonging to a teenage boy who may or may not be mine.

For those days when there is an exceptionally long wait in the carpool line, we have the home office. It's situated in the plasti-form compartments of the driver's door, which hold note pads, pens, pencils, school directories, some seven-year-old road maps that I'll never use, and a series of "Learn French in Your Car" CDs.

The seats also recline, if I'm ever in need of a bedroom. We paid extra for that feature.

In addition, there's the miscellaneous clutter found in every household, namely, an Ace Hardware five dollar cash-card, a piece of paper that entitles my boys to a free Icedream from Chick-fil-A, and a stack of Bed, Bath and Beyond coupons (because they never expire).

So, if you'd like to join me in running some errands, jump in the minivan, grab a cup of coffee, and make yourself at home.

39 GRAY AND WEATHERED

I think we can agree that in American society, our decades are defined by the color of their décor.

In the '70s, homes were decorated in burnt orange and avocado green. In the '80s, it was taupe and mauve. In the '90s, I wasn't paying attention and I have no idea what was supposed to be the "in" thing. I did, however, notice "shabby chic" start creeping into the pages of ladies' magazines and onto the shelves of Target, and I do think that this particular style sensibility has paved the way to our current color void.

Because the defining colors of this decade, as far as I can determine, are *gray* and *weathered*…with white accents.

Come on, people! Can't we do better than that? Why are we coloring our hair and lubricating our skin if we are going to decorate our homes in "gray" and "weathered"? So that we can look good in comparison?

Don't believe me? Go ahead—check a bridal registry, any bridal registry. All the dishes on offer are white—and not just shades of white, mind you, but pure white. The variety comes in the shapes. You might have square white dishes, round white dishes, curvy white dishes; you will have nuances of shapes that will challenge your powers of discernment. But all the dishes will be white.

I'm telling you, folks, plain is "in." White is the new Wedgewood. At the same time, Riedel is the new Waterford, and the blander, the better.

Still not convinced? Walk into a Restoration Hardware (but don't wear fuchsia—you'll be kicked out). I've seen more color in a game of Battleship. The store's color palate for upholstery ranges from light neutral to dark neutral. You can choose between "sand" and "fog" for your wingbacks…and you can stray as far as "mocha."

There might be an item—a pillow, perhaps—that once contained color, but it has been stripped of it so as to look stylishly dull. Thus, the pillows in the store that I used to covet due to their singular ability to lend festive splashes of color to my solid leather sofa have all been covered in burlap sacks. (But they have French words on them! And yes, that costs extra.)

Flowers are dried, furniture is distressed, linens are faded, and they all come that way when you buy them. The more worn-out it looks, the more in it is.

But I happen to like a bit of fresh color. Am I the only one left who does? Unpretentiously bold orange pumpkins, festive red ribbons tied onto evergreen garland, cheery yellow sunflowers—I think that they all serve to brighten our lives. So how is it that color has become unfashionable? Why do we only go for the vivid blues and reds when they're enameled onto a $350.00 cast-iron pot?

I'm a bit unconventional, and I've always been about two steps behind the current fashion trends, anyway. Come over to my house for lunch, and you will be served on rebelliously multicolored dishes. Because I do think that if we're honest with ourselves, we know that we can manage to use color and be tasteful at the same time. So be daring, be flamboyant, be *intense*...pull out that old, violently patterned throw you've been hiding in the basement and slap it right down onto your beige sofa.

I won't judge you.

40 THE UBERS AMONG US

I pulled something out of the pocket of a jacket I hadn't worn since last season. I know you've had that serendipitous experience, of discovering perhaps a forgotten ten-dollar bill or a Werther's Original caramel that had been stuffed into a piece of clothing. But that's not what was in my pocket. It was an old list.

I find them everywhere—lists in my purse, lists on my nightstand, lists under my lists. You see, I am a compulsive list-maker. I know I'm not the only one.

There are those who are list-makers and those who are

not list-makers, and then there are those who are uber list-makers—the truly OCD among us—like me. I am an uber.

If you're not a list-maker, you're not, and you know you're not. You're one of those happy-go-lucky, "que sera, sera" people who skip through life not worrying, being happy. What you don't know is that you've been missing out. You don't know the little tingle, the small rush, the spark of joy you get when you cross off an item on your list. It's a cheap thrill, but it's still a thrill.

If you *are* a list-maker, you know that, too. What you may not know is the difference between yourself and an uber. I am here to illuminate the distinctions.

If you are a garden-variety list-maker, you will take the time to jot down the specific groceries you intend to buy or the items you need at the hardware store. You might make a note on your smartThing, reminding yourself to take the dog to the vet or that you need to update your tetanus shot. But you will be able to function normally without a list.

If you are an uber, you cannot.

Your day will not truly begin until you have a list. List-less, you will wander aimlessly through the kitchen, coffee cup in hand, wondering what you are supposed to do until you see, let's say, a newspaper begging to be read. That will jolt you into action, so you will find a stray piece of paper and write down "read the newspaper," along with nine other tasks, and you can start your day.

If you are an uber, you will then prioritize the jobs, and if you are an advanced uber you will also designate the time periods within the day during which the jobs will take place. If you happen to complete a task that wasn't yet written on the list, you will write it down just for the satisfaction of crossing it off again. You know you're an uber if you need that fix.

If you are an uber, you will take one task and break it down into multiple steps, i.e., write the letter, address the envelope, stamp the envelope, mail the envelope. This allows for optimal crossing-off satisfaction.

If you are an uber, you will throw a little party for yourself if you actually complete everything on your list.

I hope you have been enlightened as to the differences among us. Now, if you are an uber, please cross this off your list and go about your day.

41 TUCK, TUCK, LOOSE?

I'm not exactly fashion-forward. My wardrobe is basically dictated by what I can find that fits me and is on sale, so it's a limited collection. But there's a trend I've noticed while Windows shopping during lunchtime, and in fact it's been around and persistently gaining momentum for the last few years. It's the half-tuck. You might know it by another name, as it's the style formally known as the front-tuck.

You see, once upon a time, there were two ways to wear a shirt: 1) tucked in, or 2) not.

Then a new fashion crept upon the scene, steadily increasing in popularity, until it earned its own name, i.e., the Front Tuck. The Front Tuck is a somewhat self-explanatory style that involves wearing a loose shirt and tucking in only the front of it.

The Front Tuck has a sister called the Side Tuck, which is what happens when only one-half of a buttoned-down shirt is tucked in.

Then the Tuck family grew and all kinds of Tucks were born: the Back Tuck, the Casual Tuck, the Tight Tuck, the Loose Tuck, the Twist-n-Tuck, the Wrap-n-Tuck. And, as often happens in large families, people started calling these tucklings by the same name. So the Front Tuck is also called the Half Tuck or the Casual Tuck, which leaves the Half Tuck with nothing to be called but the Half Half Tuck or the Full Gainer.

It took me a while to catch on. For the longest time, I noticed the J. Crew catalogue models wearing their tops only partly tucked, and I actually thought they were advertising their belts.

But let's get back to the front-tuck/half-tuck, remembering all the while of course, that I am *not* a stylist—I only watch them on YouTube—so I am not doling out fashion advice, I am merely passing along what I have gleaned. My understanding is that this sassy, part-in, part-out, non-comital tuck is designed to give your shirt a split personality (kind of like Superman when he takes off his glasses) by making it look professional in the front and all crazy in the back. If you do it right, you have a neatly tucked bit of shirt somewhere along the front of your jeans and a free-flowing fiesta of fabric elsewhere, which announces to everyone that you are NOT a geek, but a slave to fashion.

You might be wondering, how much tuck does a person tuck if a person could half-tuck? Rest assured that you can google "mastering the half-tuck" and find a plethora of internet tutorials on how to achieve this casual, carefree look.

If, however, you google "back-tuck," you will find videos of a gymnastic move.

It doesn't work on me. I'm either all in or all out. Oh, I tried. I watched the tutorials and worked with my forefinger and my cotton-blend fabric, spending way more time dressing myself than truly necessary, in an attempt to make my shirt display just the right amount of attitude. But I never arrived at "jaunty," I only accomplished "disheveled." I might make a belt-wink with my shirt, but that ends up sloppy, too.

So I've concluded that until this fashion trend plays out, I'll just stick with dresses.

42 THE FLAW

My daughter breaks the mold. She cooks and cleans without being asked, she plays catch with her younger brothers, and she has made it clear through adolescence with nary an incident of "drama." Plus, she's kind to animals and small children.

But all this goodness comes at a price: she doesn't like to shop.

Signs of The Flaw began to appear around the age of five. My mother took her shopping and tried to buy her an adorable dress that had been marked down twice. As the story goes, my mother continued to coax her into the dress and finally relented, saying, "Sweetie, if I buy this for you, you won't wear it, will you?"

"No, grandma," my daughter replied with a shake of her head, "and that will be your punishment."

Your *punishment?!* My stars, child! Have I taught you nothing about gift horses?

Apparently not.

I still have to bribe her to buy clothes, even now that she's grown into a long-legged, model–sized coed. "Here, honey, get this dress, it looks fantastic on you! If you let me buy this for you, I won't ask you to let me buy anything else for you for the rest of the year! I promise!"

It's no fun at all.

Plus, I can't take her shopping with me—it's like shopping with a sixty-two year old man. She's kind of a killjoy.

"Honey, how do like this dress on me?"

"It's great. How much is it?"

"Sweetie, that's not a question you need to ask. Do you like it?"

"When would you wear it?"

"You don't understand clothes shopping at all, do you? How about these pants?"

"Don't you already have black pants?"

"Yes, dear, but that's not the point."

She doesn't understand that having only one pair of

black pants is like having only one song from your favorite band. Mumford and Sons' "Little Lion Man" sounds an awful lot like their "I Will Wait," but I still want them both.

Worse than that, The Flaw stymies her sense of color and fashion. She doesn't get that she can have the black pump *and* the navy slingbacks—they don't cancel each other out.

To make matters more frustrating, she wears a size 8 shoe, that template of shoes, that size that every possible design comes in, so she has a dizzying array of choices, while I on the other hand, who get all tingly and teary-eyed over a great pair of shoes, wear a size 5.

We'll walk into a DSW, she'll make a beeline for the sales racks in the back of the store, and there will be rows upon rows of size 8s. I need to stop and eat a small snack by the time I've found my way clear of the 8s and into the 7s. Even then, I can only find the size 5s by scouting around until I see a small clump of tiny women huddled over a purple shoe.

That'll be where I discover the quarter of a row that holds a meager two shelves of size 5 shoes (which are mixed together with the 4s and the 5½s, by the way), and they are all made of fur.

Meanwhile, my daughter has a choice between thirteen different styles of tan wedges, and she doesn't buy any of them.

There is no fairness in the world.

So, we return home from a typical shopping spree with a pair of size 8 blacks flats, size 5 zebra-patterned slippers, and my forth pair of black pants. Then I'll retire to the den to nurse my headache, and my daughter will get dinner started.

43 THE NAME GAME

I finally decided to follow my son's Tumblr account, seeing as he's currently on the other side of the globe and at one point interviewed the opposition leader in some sort of uprising in Macedonia.

His activities piqued my interest enough for me to make the effort to logon to his social media account and sign up.

And what an effort it was! Usually it's my password that doesn't pass muster, which is why I now have approximately forty-three variations on my original (six-letter/one digit) password-of-choice, each with a slight deviation of capitals, digits, and letters, and therefore all now completely impossible to recall. But again, this time I was able to slip by easily with my newly updated, back-up, eight-letter/one-digit password-of-choice (which I will still probably forget). This time, it was the username that got me.

Of course "robin" wouldn't work—I didn't even attempt that. But I had created a handy new username, "alwayswrite," that I have used before on other sites and considered somewhat clever in a punny sort of way, and which I can actually remember.

So I keyed it in, but that one was taken. I could choose "I-alwayswrite-blog," which completely loses the pun, or "awesomealwayswritelove," which is an awful username. So, no.

I could also choose "youralwayswrite," which I would never, ever do, because *your* in this case should actually be the contraction *you're*, and I would rather melt my keyboard into a useless metal blob than choose a username that so defiles one of the most basic grammar rules. I could, of course, revise the name to read "youralwayswritemother," but that also blows the pun right out the window. So, no.

The feeble flicker of username creativity that I possess had already been expunged upon the name "alwayswrite," so I looked around for inspiration. My geraniums are still in bloom in the blue pot on my back deck, so I typed in "geranium." I was stunned to be informed that "someone has already claimed your username," even when it was so completely random, and I was offered the names "geranium-things," "a-geranium," (both of which are stupid, I'm sure you agree), and "omg-geranium," which is not only stupid, but juvenile. So, no.

Throughout this exercise, however, the Tumblr site offered me a collection of new and unsullied usernames, such as "SecretPhilosopherBouquet" and "AtomicBluebirdFart," which were admittedly tempting, but didn't quite feel right. So, no.

Still on the flower theme, I tried "honeysucklerose," but that was also taken. I could be "bat-honeysucklerose," which doesn't even make sense, or "honeysucklerose-stuff," which is equally inane. No, and no. Tumblr, meanwhile, offered me "TenaciousFuryStudent" and "UnadulteratedNinjamoon," but neither of those really define me, so, no.

I was getting testy now. Our ample bowlful of Halloween candy prompted me to go all-out with "99%chocolate," a name which not only describes my diet, but also my favorite Lindt chocolate bar. I came awfully close with that one, but was informed that "Tumblrname can only contain letters, numbers, and dashes," although I could choose "omg99chocolateblog," which again, for reasons mentioned, I would never do.

On the suggestion of one of my twins, I typed in "99chocolate" and was finally admitted to an entirely new page, but then demurred, because I was not ready to abandon the qualifying %. So I backtracked and of course had to start all over again.

But I was rewarded with a new offering: "Teenage-DoughnutEarthquake," which my own teenage son thought fit me perfectly and which convinced me that checking out username suggestions on Tumblr could become a habit.

Committed to my username decision, I typed in "99percentchocolate," which did indeed and at last work. But now I was forced to reveal my age (because Tumblr did not accept "old enough" and because I cannot tell a lie, not even to Tumblr). I then assured Tumblr that I am not a robot, and that was all it needed to know in order to present me with a veritable landslide of Tumblr accounts prime for the following.

It doesn't understand—I'm only here to follow my son.

44 IS IT TIME TO RETREAT FROM TRICK OR TREAT?

I used to cringe at the sight of groups of large and lanky teenagers trolling the neighborhood with pillowcases on Halloween night. *Greedy, candy-grubbing twerps*, I used to think, picking out the smallest, cheapest bits of sweet tarts from my bowl and handing over one piece each to six-foot-tall boys wearing "I heart Bacon" T-shirts and giggly girls in Catwoman ears.

But things have changed. Now my kids are among the trollers. My sons are taking college-level courses in high school, but they still haven't outgrown the lure of free candy…lots and lots of free candy.

Determined *not* to be one of "those moms" who lets her teenagers run rampant through a holiday invented for preschoolers, I tried to curb it last year. It seemed to me that if you're old enough to drive a car, you're too old to trick or treat.

But I caved to peer pressure, and it came from all sides—from my boys' friends and from their friends' mothers (a.k.a. my friends). My line was outvoted.

I understood the other side of the argument: "It's just wholesome fun. It's just one night a year. They'll be too old soon." And there was indeed a persistent, albeit tiny, little voice in my head that was agreeing, *Okay, already, let them have their one night of fun. This will be the last time. Besides, it's not like they want to run off and get a tongue piercing.*

So I relented and let them go on All Hallows Eve, with a list of provisos:

*Don't keep at it after 9 p.m., and don't knock on the door if the lights are out.

*Don't carry a pillowcase, and don't grab a handful from the candy bucket.

*Try not to look so tall—slump, if you have to.

*Don't trample the flower beds.

*Be sure to say "thank you."

*And for the love of all things pumpkin, make an effort at a costume.

So out they went, to the thrill of the hunt, the last rite of childhood, the joy of free chocolate, all experienced in the camaraderie of friends.

And they had a great time.

Will they want to go out again this year? I don't know. But I have decided that if they ask to go, it's not a battle worth fighting. I'll send them off with a kiss and a flashlight. And I'll add one more item to my list of conditions: I want the Almond Joys.

45 ODE TO THE GOURD

It's November, and you know what that means: pumpkin is the new bacon.

Pumpkin is everywhere, flavoring everything from French toast to toothpaste. We've got pumpkin pancakes, pumpkin salsa, pumpkin ice cream, pumpkin beer—in fact, I think that there actually *is* a pumpkin bacon. But probably the most familiar and best loved uses of the pumpkin, at least in this country, at least at this time of year, is to make it into a pie.

Pumpkin pie was my son's favorite when he was young. I loved it too, because it was so darn easy to make. A can of pumpkin, a can of sweetened condensed milk, a frozen pie crust, and some eggs and spices were all it took for me to be the mother of the year—or at least feel like I was.

I remember one November when my little boy wanted to have pumpkin pie for breakfast, and because he was my first child, I wouldn't let him. I did, however, round up enough cans of pumpkin one May to make pumpkin pies for his entire kindergarten class for his birthday. I think I redeemed myself.

Pumpkin is one of those "what's not to love?" squashes. It's easy on the eyes and easy on the palate. It has a perky color and a pleasing shape. It's affably rotund, so we can feel trim in comparison. We know it's healthy because it grows on a farm and it's orange. We also know that we can take a brownie and stick some pumpkin in it and that makes it nutritious, and so then we can have two.

I learned to respect the pumpkin many years ago, when I was in the jack-o'-lantern stage of my motherhood. I had gathered my kids round the kitchen table, and we gutted the gourd and ripped out its slimy innards. We managed to carve a crooked face into the thing—face enough for the candlelight to flicker through on Halloween.

The pumpkin shone on its night of glory, and then (harried mother that I was), I let it sit there and sit there until it became a true horror figure in its own right. I finally rolled it off onto the unkempt square of yard at the end of our driveway and forgot about it as it became covered with leaves and frost and slowly, grossly, disintegrated.

The following spring, there was a pumpkin patch growing in its place. It was the revenge of the gourd.

Not only is it resilient, the pumpkin is versatile. It can be a door stop, a centerpiece, or a soup bowl. It's got something for everyone. We can carve it, light it, chuck it, smash it, roast it, mash it, and turn it into risotto.

Now we're in high pumpkin season. If turkey is the star of the Thanksgiving table, pumpkin is the best supporting actor. I've got a cornucopia full of pumpkins on the dining room table and two metal pumpkins decorating our deck. I've got a pumpkin cheesecake in the freezer, a pumpkin-shaped muffin tin in the cabinet waiting for batter, and a sweet little pumpkin on my counter that will eventually become a pie.

My son's coming home for Thanksgiving, and he'll get a big slice of it.

It's what's for breakfast.

46 A DAY OF PURÉE

Someone, in fact, *did* say it would be easy. Blogs, books, and food network throw-downs abound regarding the mindless simplicity of making your own pumpkin purée.

Why, a Boy Scout with a pocket knife and old set of bicycle gears could do it.

I saw photos of the process—step-by-step instructions—where 1) docile pumpkins lay in wait, 2) are cooked, 3) their cooked skin practically rolls itself off its own pulp, and 4) the pulp blends beautifully. In the time it takes to file your nails, you could produce a batch of smooth and vibrantly colored purée that would be fresh with flavor and bursting with vitamin A. It would be so much tastier than that brownish orange *glop* that comes out of a can.

Yes, according to the blogs, the nutrition-to-ease ratio is roughly five-to-one in favor of going for it. I should have known better because the truth is, I'm not that great in the kitchen. I'm famous in my house for burning water.

But I'm a farm-to-table kind of gal, so go for it, I did.

I bought two pie pumpkins, one of which happened to be organic. I did a quick calculation of the cost and estimated that for the same amount of money, I could have purchased a case of Libby's canned pumpkin—or a completely baked pie.

Home I went. After only about an hour, the pumpkins were sliced and gutted, their slimy, stringy seeds in a large bowl of water, awaiting the next farm-to-table treatment. I decided that roasting the pumpkins would be the simplest cooking method, so I lined up slices on a cookie sheet and shoved it in the oven.

Soon, my house was filled with the healthy smell of squash.

The slices were supposed to roast for forty-five minutes, but my oven was not cooperating. It has digital controls, of course, and extremely sensitive ones, which means that if I so much as stand next to it and sneeze, it turns off. The pumpkin had been in the oven for thirty minutes when I realized that the oven had—at some point—stopped heating. I was beginning to get impatient, and steaming was supposed to be faster, so I crawled under my kitchen cabinet, pulled out my stock pot, and dumped the entire batch of pumpkin pieces into the steamer basket.

I was clocking into my third hour of partying with the pumpkins, and they still weren't done. I didn't care—I was ready to get this over with and go shoe shopping.

The skins that had peeled off so effortlessly in the photos were clinging to the pulp the way a woman clings to her purse on a New York subway, and I whittled them off, inch by inch, and threw yellowish chunks of pumpkin into the food processor. My processer wasn't machine enough for the job, though, and large masses of squash refused to be pulverized. So I pulled out my blender. I was puréeing my second batch of the stuff around the time my kids started asking what was for dinner.

Finally, during hour four, I puréed my last batch, wondering all the while what my neighbors were doing on this beautiful afternoon three days before Thanksgiving. I surveyed my kitchen. There was a dirty food processor, an orange goo-coated blender, a cookie sheet covered with sticky pumpkin seeds, a stock pot on the stove, and a counter filled with pumpkin parts. I had produced four cups of bright orange...*glop*. It was filled with pumpkin strings, bits of rind, and chunks of unpuréed pumpkin.

Well. You don't find THAT in a can! It was of questionable consistency. The batch of it wouldn't matter if it were on its way to becoming risotto, but as the featured ingredient of a pumpkin-shaped muffin, it mattered.

The muffins came out cute and properly formed, but were missing a certain something, a key element...that robust flavor of *pumpkin* that comes conveniently out of a can. I called them "spice cakes" and roasted the seeds.

And the seeds were good.

47   FRIENDSGIVING

I was at the salon a few weeks ago for my seasonal haircut, engaging in mindless chit-chat with the cute young gal who was washing my hair, when she asked me about my plans for the Thanksgiving weekend.

"Well, we have a pre-Thanksgiving chili night with neighbors on the Wednesday before Thanksgiving," I began.

She, being under thirty and thus recognizing all things "trending," perked up and said, "Oh! You're having a Friendsgiving!"

"No," I frowned, admitting to my own un-trending-ness. "It's pre-Thanksgiving Chili Night with Neighbors."

I won't have my fun chili night labeled by a trendy cliché.

Friendsgiving, for those of you who are as un-trending as I am, is marketed as Thanksgiving, only better. A snarkier definition is that it's a Thanksgiving meal ostensibly shared with people you really WANT to eat with instead of with the people you really DON'T want to eat with...or something like that. It can happen anytime during the month of November: the Wednesday before or the Friday after, the weekend after, or really any day at all except on Thanksgiving...no, it can even happen on Thanksgiving.

Friendsgiving has its own invitations, Pinterest pages, Wiki page, and page on Miriam-Webster.com. It has its own set of rules on Buzzfeed and The Kitchn, created by people who write for Buzzfeed and The Kitchn. (Here I digress just long enough to wholeheartedly endorse a rule listed on both sites which states that if you are assigned to bring a dish, bring it completely prepared—do not bring its components and assemble it in the host's kitchen. Thank you, Social Network site writers, for validating my personal pet peeve.)

Southern Living has even gotten into the game, devoting a post to Friendsgiving recipes that look suspiciously like Thanksgiving recipes.

So maybe our pre-Thanksgiving Chili Night with Neighbors doesn't qualify as Friendsgiving anyway, because we don't do the traditional turkey and sides. Either way, I like our plan much better. I have enough trouble cooking one turkey a year; I don't want to do two in one month. Besides that, it will be July, and I will still manage to discover a Tupperware container of leftover turkey or sweet potato casserole in the back of the freezer—I don't need more of the same from an identical dinner. Like a Disney side-kick, a bowl of chili provides a welcome relief to the barrage of leftovers on the one end and the barrage of preparations on the other.

Back to our pre-Thanksgiving Chili Night with Neighbors. We take turns hosting and supplying the chili; my friend makes Cincinnati style, and I make half-time style. We also supply kids, parents, and occasional surprise guests, and we always have a great evening, unmarred by the fact that we are practically trending—but not quite.

The only other snag in our Pre-Thanksgiving Chili Night with Neighbors is the clunky title. I admit that "Friendsgiving" is a whole lot catchier. So what shall we call it? "Chili Night" is too generic. "No Thanks-giving" is too harsh. Thanks Con Carne? Three Alarm Neighbors? Friends Five Ways?

Let me know, and I'll start my own trend.

48 UNITED BY AN APRON

I'm a sucker for an apron.

I can slip on an apron that has a fetching Provincial pattern and imagine myself domestically stylish.

I used to never wear aprons—I thought them too retro and frumpy. Fortunately, now retro is in and aprons are chic. When I had finally ruined favorite shirt number thirty-four with a wayward splash of olive oil, I decided that it was time to tie one on.

And tie one on I do—every day—usually around three o'clock, as I a grab a cup of tea and drive off to the carpool line. I keep it on for the red wine I sip while chopping onions, and I wear it straight through dinner and into cleanup.

It's typically ten o'clock before I disrobe.

So, when I ran into my favorite kitchen shop last week to purchase my annual indulgence of harvest-scented hand soap and saw the Thanksgiving apron on display, I didn't stand a chance. It was a lovely shade of autumn gold with a curly-stemmed pumpkin tastefully embroidered on the front. It had a handy row of deep pockets and an adjustable strap. Plus, it was 20 percent off.

I tried it on, thinking of what an extra boost of classy confidence this little frock would lend to my turkey and side-dish preparations. I thought it would make a fine, if practical, mini-splurge for my upcoming November birthday. Then, something tugged on the apron strings....

Maybe I could get one for my mom, too.

Because this year is different. My parents have spent the last several years in Florida during the Thanksgiving holidays. But in July, my wonderful father succumbed to cancer; this year, my mother is staying in Atlanta. She will be spending Thanksgiving with us.

Whenever my mother comes to my home, she goes immediately to the kitchen and stands at my side to help. Yes, I would get a Thanksgiving apron for my mom, too. Then I felt another tug....

Maybe I could get one for my daughter, as well.

Maybe this apron could be more than a pretty piece of protective fabric. Maybe, when worn by the trio of us, it could signify something else. Maybe it can be the beginning of a new tradition: three generations of women gathered as a Thanksgiving team. We will embrace each other and work together, and we will celebrate in honor of my dad, in gratitude for his life and his legacy.

This November, my family and my mother will come to the Thanksgiving table for the first time ever without our beloved father, and grandfather, and husband. We will share sorrow, and remembrance, and comfort food. We will begin a new tradition.

And, we will be united by an apron.

WINTER

ACKNOWLEDGMENTS

To my son Robby, who encouraged me to write a few columns and peddle them the old-fashioned way; to my daughter Katie, who serves as a keen editorial first-reader; to my son Nick, who is a relief editor; and to my son Michael, who always keeps good humor while I am losing mine—thank you, you are wonderful, and I can't believe that I gave birth to you.

I am tremdously grateful to my publisher, Steve Levene, who envisioned this collection around the same time I did and who worked with and supported me in the creation of this book.

I am immensely grateful as well to the unflappable Joe Earle, who took a chance on me and endorsed me as a columnist for the Reporter Newspapers, who also cleaned up this manuscript, and who has enough respect for the printed word to spend a considerable amount of editorial time debating about an adjective.

I offer my sincere thanks and admiration to John Ruch, Kathy Dean, and to the staff and board of the Reporter Newspapers and Atlanta Senior Life. I am particularly grateful to Soojin Yang for her meticulous work on the body of this manuscript and for her brilliant graphic designs.

I am also truly appreciative of my dear friends and family for feedback and enthusiastic support.

Most especially, I thank my husband, Lou, who has provided encouragement, critique, wise counsel, and constant love for three decades of my life.

A CHRISTMAS EVOLUTION

This December, as I wrestle with my holiday nemesis—the faux green garland monstrosity that I try to whack into submission and hang on my banister each year—I'm reminded of a simpler time when gifts were modest and decorations were tame and filled but one plastic storage container.

That time was when we were first married. He gave me wool socks and an inflatable camping mattress pad. (Are you picking up on a theme?) I gave him a tweed hat. My best friend gave us a pair of mugs painted with a couple that kissed each other when the mugs were arranged just so. We each had a stocking. Mine was quilted and lace-trimmed, a gift from my former roommate; his was a red felt version purchased from a mall kiosk with his name written on it in tacky red glitter. There was a crystal ornament from my parents that said "Our first Christmas together."

That was about it.

Our family grew and things changed. There came the pregnant lady ornament, the Baby's First Christmas ornament, the set of Pokémon ornaments. With each child came more stockings, stockings of all kinds from relatives of all sorts. And with each child came more ornaments, ornaments of all kinds from relatives of all sorts. I added angels and nutcrackers to the stockings and ornaments. I augmented with wreathes and stars. I began to feature a nativity scene in every room.

Some people have all of their decorations in "the box." I have accumulated enough boxes of Christmas stuff to decorate the country of Liechtenstein.

As our family grew, the gifts changed, too. One minute, I was waving a multi-purpose rattle in front of my infant's face, and before I knew it, I was standing at the Toys-R-Us in a line so long and studded with security guards that you'd think Bono was at the other end of it.

I see the remnants and recall the years.

There is the Goofy doll in a Santa suit. It was a gift from the nurses at our local hospital, where my daughter spent her first Christmas Eve with a raging upper respiratory infection. There is, believe it or not, a set of encyclopedias lined up neatly on the basement bookshelves, given years ago to my first son—who still prefers hard copy, God bless him.

There is an old remote wired to the TV, from the year that I was awakened at 6:30 a.m. in mid-December by a phone call from a friend; she had insider information that Costco was getting a shipment of Wiis. She picked me up and drove us there, where we waited with a small crowd outside the building while clinging to our venti lattes. I remember looking around at the other bleary-eyed mothers and thinking to myself, they weren't there for the poinsettias.

Our kids are getting older, and the day after Thanksgiving no longer marks the beginning of gift-hunting season for me. Still, I'll find them a few things.

One son needs clothes, and he likes what I buy for him. One son wants a Tesla coil, and I do admire that particular, scientific wish. His twin never asks for anything, but he really likes bacon…and I did hear about a "bacon of the month" club. And my daughter has refused to buy herself new shoes for two years, so it's time for me to intervene.

They all still like chocolate oranges, and Santa will still put toothbrushes in their stockings.

I look around the house. The faux green garland is clinging to the bannister. My angels are on the mantle, my nutcrackers are on the sideboard, there are stockings hanging all over the place. The kissing mugs are in the kitchen.

And after thirty years together, he still wears the hat and I still wear the socks.